AF841938

ECONOMIC ISSUES, PROBLEMS AND PERSPECTIVES

TRENDS IN THE ECONOMIC WELL-BEING OF FEMALE-HEADED HOUSEHOLDS

Economic Issues, Problems and Perspectives

Additional books in this series can be found on Nova's website
under the Series tab.

Additional E-books in this series can be found on Nova's website
under the E-book tab.

ECONOMIC ISSUES, PROBLEMS AND PERSPECTIVES

TRENDS IN THE ECONOMIC WELL-BEING OF FEMALE-HEADED HOUSEHOLDS

GABRIELLE YOUNG
AND
DONALD T. GREEN
EDITORS

Nova Science Publishers, Inc.
New York

Copyright © 2012 by Nova Science Publishers, Inc.

All rights reserved. No part of this book may be reproduced, stored in a retrieval system or transmitted in any form or by any means: electronic, electrostatic, magnetic, tape, mechanical photocopying, recording or otherwise without the written permission of the Publisher.

For permission to use material from this book please contact us:
Telephone 631-231-7269; Fax 631-231-8175
Web Site: http://www.novapublishers.com

NOTICE TO THE READER

The Publisher has taken reasonable care in the preparation of this book, but makes no expressed or implied warranty of any kind and assumes no responsibility for any errors or omissions. No liability is assumed for incidental or consequential damages in connection with or arising out of information contained in this book. The Publisher shall not be liable for any special, consequential, or exemplary damages resulting, in whole or in part, from the readers' use of, or reliance upon, this material. Any parts of this book based on government reports are so indicated and copyright is claimed for those parts to the extent applicable to compilations of such works.

Independent verification should be sought for any data, advice or recommendations contained in this book. In addition, no responsibility is assumed by the publisher for any injury and/or damage to persons or property arising from any methods, products, instructions, ideas or otherwise contained in this publication.

This publication is designed to provide accurate and authoritative information with regard to the subject matter covered herein. It is sold with the clear understanding that the Publisher is not engaged in rendering legal or any other professional services. If legal or any other expert assistance is required, the services of a competent person should be sought. FROM A DECLARATION OF PARTICIPANTS JOINTLY ADOPTED BY A COMMITTEE OF THE AMERICAN BAR ASSOCIATION AND A COMMITTEE OF PUBLISHERS.
Additional color graphics may be available in the e-book version of this book.

LIBRARY OF CONGRESS CATALOGING-IN-PUBLICATION DATA

Trends in the economic well-being of female-headed households / editors, Gabrielle Young and Donald T. Green.
p. cm.
Includes index.
ISBN 978-1-62100-931-3 (hardcover)
1. Women heads of households--United States. 2. Fatherless families--United States. 3. Single mothers--United States--Economic conditions. 4. Welfare recipients--Employment--United States. 5. Public welfare--United States. I. Young, Gabrielle. II. Green, Donald T.
HV700.5.T74 2011
362.830973--dc23

2011040390

Published by Nova Science Publishers, Inc. † New York

CONTENTS

PREFACE

It is almost 15 years since repeal of what was the nation's major cash welfare program assisting low-income families with children, the Aid to Families with Dependent Children (AFDC) program, and its replacement with a block grant of Temporary Assistance for Needy Families (TANF). This book focuses on trends in the economic well-being of female-headed families with children, the principal group affected by the replacement of AFDC with TANF.

Chapter 1 - It is almost 15 years since repeal of what was the nation's major cash welfare program assisting low-income families with children, the Aid to Families with Dependent Children (AFDC) program, and its replacement with a block grant of Temporary Assistance for Needy Families (TANF). This report focuses on trends in the economic well-being of female-headed families with children, the principal group affected by the replacement of AFDC with TANF. Female-headed families and their children are especially at risk of poverty, and children in such families account for well over half of all poor children in the United States. For these reasons, single female-headed families continue to be of particular concern to policymakers. The report details trends in income and poverty status of these families, prior and subsequent to enactment of the 1996 welfare reform law and other policy changes. The report focuses especially on welfare dependency and work engagement among single mothers, a major dynamic that welfare reform and accompanying policy changes have attempted to affect. It also examines the role of programs other than TANF in providing support to single female-headed families with children.

Chapter 2 - The Temporary Assistance for Needy Families (TANF) program, created in 1996, is one of the key federal funding streams provided to states to assist women and children in poverty. A critical aspect of TANF has been its focus on employment and self-sufficiency, and the primary means to measure state efforts in this area has been TANF's work participation rate requirements. Legislative changes in 2005 were generally expected to strengthen these work requirements. Given changes in the number of families participating in TANF over time and questions about whether the program is achieving its goals, this testimony draws on previous GAO work to focus on 1) key changes to state welfare programs made in response to TANF and other legislation and their effect on caseload trends; 2) how low-income single-parent families are faring; and 3) how recent developments in state programs and the economy may affect federal monitoring of TANF. To address these issues, in previous work conducted from November 2008 to May 2010, GAO analyzed state data reported to the Department of Health and Human Services; used microsimulation analyses; surveyed state TANF administrators in 50 states and the District of Columbia; interviewed officials in 21 states selected to represent a range of economic conditions and TANF policy decisions; conducted site visits to Florida, Ohio, and Oregon; and reviewed relevant federal laws, regulations, and research.

In: Trends in the Economic Well-Being … ISBN: 978-1-62100-931-3
Eds.: G. Young and D. T. Green © 2012 Nova Science Publishers, Inc.

Chapter 1

WELFARE, WORK, AND POVERTY STATUS OF FEMALE-HEADED FAMILIES WITH CHILDREN: 1987-2009

Thomas Gabe

SUMMARY

It is almost 15 years since repeal of what was the nation's major cash welfare program assisting low-income families with children, the Aid to Families with Dependent Children (AFDC) program, and its replacement with a block grant of Temporary Assistance for Needy Families (TANF). This report focuses on trends in the economic well-being of female-headed families with children, the principal group affected by the replacement of AFDC with TANF. Female-headed families and their children are especially at risk of poverty, and children in such families account for well over half of all poor children in the United States. For these reasons, single female-headed families continue to be of particular concern to policymakers. The report details trends in income and poverty status of these families, prior and subsequent to enactment of the 1996 welfare reform law and other policy changes. The report focuses especially on welfare dependency and work engagement among single mothers, a major dynamic that welfare reform and accompanying policy changes have attempted to affect. It also examines the role of programs other than TANF in providing support to single female-headed families with children.

CRS analysis of 23 years of U.S. Census Bureau data shows that there has been a dramatic transformation with regard to welfare, work, and poverty status of single mothers. The period has seen a marked *structural change* in the provision of benefits under a number of programs that contribute to the fabric of the nation's "income safety net." In turn, single mothers' *behavior has changed* markedly over the period; more mothers are working and fewer are relying on cash welfare to support themselves and their children.

In the years immediately preceding 1996 welfare reform, and in the years since, the nation's income safety net has been transformed into one supporting work. Cash-welfare work requirements, the end of cash welfare as an open-ended entitlement by limiting the duration that individuals may receive federally funded benefits, and expanded earnings and family income supplements administered through the federal income tax system have helped to change the dynamics between work and welfare. The transformed system has helped to both reduce single mothers' reliance on traditional cash welfare and reduce poverty among their children.

Poverty under the official U.S. poverty measure, which is based on pre-tax cash income, shows that since 2000, which marked an historical low, the poverty rate among single mothers has increased in step with two recessions. In 2009, the official poverty rate for single mothers, at a post-2000 high, was still below pre-1996 welfare reform levels despite two recessions. Using a more comprehensive income definition than that used by the official poverty measure indicates that poverty among single mothers and their children in 2009, rather than having increased since 2000, was at or near a 23-year low when Food Stamp/SNAP benefits and work-related refundable tax credits are taken into account. These programs' anti-poverty effects go unnoticed under the official U.S. measure. Congressional action in response to the recession, which increased SNAP benefits and extended the reach of refundable tax credits, contributed to a decline in poverty among single mothers and their children. Use of an expanded income poverty measure highlights effects of congressional action that helped reduce child poverty amidst the deepest and longest recession since the Great Depression. Some of the provisions that helped to reduce child poverty are due to expire at the end of 2012.

The role of work-conditioned benefits, and the provision of traditional cash welfare, will likely come under increased attention given the slow pace of economic recovery, the federal and state budget deficits, and a dearth of jobs.

INTRODUCTION

It is almost 15 years since repeal of what was the nation's major cash welfare program assisting low-income families with children, the Aid to Families with Dependent Children (AFDC) program, and its replacement with a block grant of Temporary Assistance for Needy Families (TANF). This report focuses on trends in the economic well-being of female-headed families with children, the principal group affected by the replacement of AFDC with TANF. Female-headed families and their children are especially at risk of poverty, and children in such families account for well over half of all poor children in the United States. For these reasons, single female-headed families continue to be of particular concern to policymakers. The report details trends in income and poverty status of these families, prior and subsequent to enactment of the 1996 welfare reform law and other policy changes. The report focuses especially on welfare dependency and work engagement among single mothers, a major dynamic that welfare reform and accompanying policy changes have attempted to affect. It also examines the role of programs other than TANF in providing support to single female-headed families with children.

Since at least the first White House Conference on Children in 1909 (Conference on the Care of Dependent Children), and the subsequent creation of the Children's Bureau in 1912, the federal government has been concerned with the social conditions of children. The Conference was an impetus for states' enactment of state or locally financed mothers' pensions (also referred to as widows' pensions and/or mothers' aid), which provided minimal cash support to mothers made destitute, usually due to a husband's death. Mothers' aid was intended to help keep the mother at home to care for her children, as an alternative to institutionalization or adoption. As part of the Social Security Act of 1935, the federal Aid to Dependent Children (ADC) program introduced federal involvement in helping provide financial aid, or "public assistance," to aid dependent children, basically as a supplement to states' mothers' pension programs. Federal involvement in attempting to address the problem of child poverty associated with the loss of parental support grew over the next 61 years, at which point the AFDC program, formerly named ADC, was repealed and replaced by Temporary Assistance for Needy Families (TANF).

Two dominant, often conflicting, themes have pervaded public discourse and policy responses to providing public assistance to poor families with children. One has been to help improve the economic and social well-being of children who, through no fault of their own, live in poor circumstances. The other has been reducing welfare dependency. A persistent challenge has been how public policy and programs can address the first theme of reducing child poverty without undermining the second by encouraging welfare dependency. A major goal of social policy over at least the past 45 years, since passage of the 1967 Social Security Act welfare amendments, has been to reduce welfare dependency and, as a consequence, child poverty, by encouraging work. This report focuses on the results of efforts to attain these goals, focusing on female-headed families with children.

CRS analysis of 23 years of U.S. Census Bureau data[1] presented in this report shows a dramatic transformation in single mothers' welfare, work, and poverty status over the period. The period examined encompasses a fundamental transformation in the provision of income support through cash welfare to a system promoting and supplementing work. The period has been marked by three recessions, one in the pre-welfare reform era (1990-1991), and two after (2001; 2007-2009); the latter was so severe that it has come to be identified by many as "The Great Recession."[2] Policy interventions to both stimulate the economy and protect those most vulnerable in response to the most recent recession are examined in the context of their effects on families headed by single mothers. The 23-year period examined provides for a range of insights about social programs' and policies' effects, under varying economic conditions, on families headed by single mothers—a group at considerable risk of poverty.[3]

A Road Map

The body of the report begins with a brief discussion as to why female-headed families with children are a focus of policy concern. Most directly, children living in such families are many times more likely to be poor than children in married-couple families. Moreover, the families in which they reside are especially likely to depend on public assistance (i.e., welfare) for at least part of their financial support.

The dual goals of reducing child poverty and breaking the bonds of welfare dependency have proven to be an enduring, and often vexing, policy challenge. The report briefly describes the policy landscape prior to 1996 welfare reform and policy changes that have occurred since—especially those that were undertaken in response to the recent recession. A brief, 100-year historical perspective as to how past policy efforts attempted to address the dual problems of child poverty and welfare dependency is presented in Appendix A.

The report then turns to an empirical analysis of trends in single mothers' work, welfare, and poverty status over the 23-year period from 1987 to 2009. Trends in the incidence of poverty and cash welfare receipt and work among single mothers are presented, as are trends in the cash welfare receipt (ADC, AFDC, and TANF) and other selected benefits. Particular attention is paid to the role of selected income sources on poverty reduction among single-mother families, overall and by whether or not mothers worked during the year. Some sources of income are not included in the "official" U.S. poverty measure, which is based on pre-tax cash income. The analysis shows that the inclusion of other income sources not included in the official measure, such as Food Stamp or Supplemental Nutrition Assistance Program (SNAP) benefits and refundable federal income tax credits, have a significant effect on poverty reduction among single mothers and their children. The inclusion of such benefits yields a very different picture as to the apparent trend in poverty, especially when viewed in the context of the most recent recession.

A final section of the report offers a concluding discussion. It highlights the transformation from income safety net to work-conditioned support, and cash welfare's resulting residual safety net role. It assesses the effectiveness of income safety net programs in reducing poverty among female-headed families, especially in the context of the recent recession and selected congressional action.

The report contains three appendices. Appendix A provides a brief history of the AFDC program—the precursor to TANF. Appendix B examines under-reporting of cash welfare on the CPS/ASEC relative to administrative benchmarks. Appendix C provides data underlying the figures presented in the body of the report.

FEMALE-HEADED FAMILIES WITH CHILDREN - A POLICY CONCERN

Two dominant, often conflicting, themes have pervaded public discourse and policy responses to providing public assistance to poor families with children. One has been to help improve the economic and social well-being of children who, through no fault of their own, live in poor circumstances. The other has been to reduce welfare dependency and to promote parental responsibility and family self sufficiency. A persistent challenge has been how public policy and programs can address the first theme of reducing child poverty without undermining the second by encouraging welfare dependency.

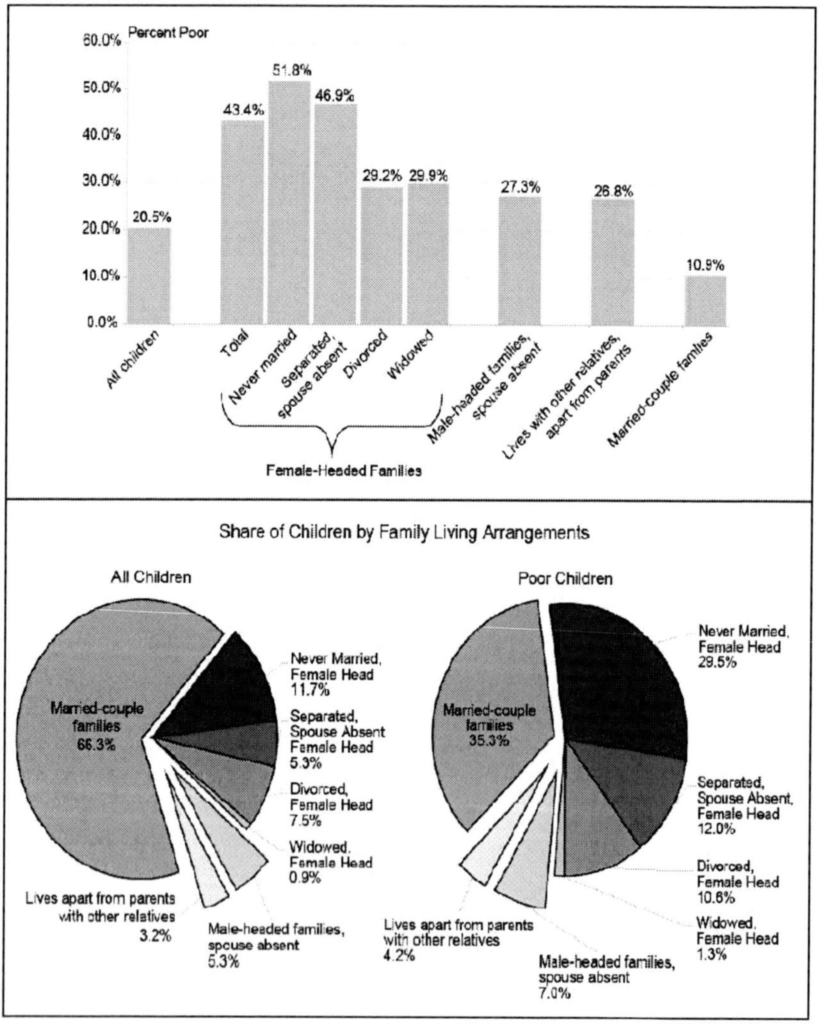

Source: Prepared by the Congressional Research Service (CRS) based on analysis of U.S. Census Bureau 2010 Current Population Survey (CPS) Annual Social and Economic Supplement (ASEC) data. See Table C-1 for supporting data.

Figure 1. Children's Poverty Status by Family Living Arrangement, 2009.

Children living in families headed by single mothers with no spouse present are especially at risk of being poor. In 2009, under the official U.S. poverty measure,[4] about one-fifth of all children were poor (20.5%), but among children living in single-mother families, over two-fifths (43.4%) were poor, compared to about one-in-nine children (10.9%) living in married-couple families (See Figure 1).[5] In 2009, one-in-four children (25.2%) lived in female-headed families, but children in such families accounted for over half (53.5%) of all poor children (see bottom panel of Figure 1). About one-in-nine children (11.7%) live in families headed by single mothers who have never been married; over half of all such children were poor in 2009 (51.8%), and they accounted for three children out of 10 (29.5%) who were poor.

Figure 2 shows the number of recipients (total, children, and adults) and cases (families, and child-only cases) receiving cash assistance under AFDC (ADC, prior to 1962) from 1960 to 1994, the eve of the 1996 welfare reform debate. The AFDC caseload was comprised almost entirely of women with no husband present and their children.

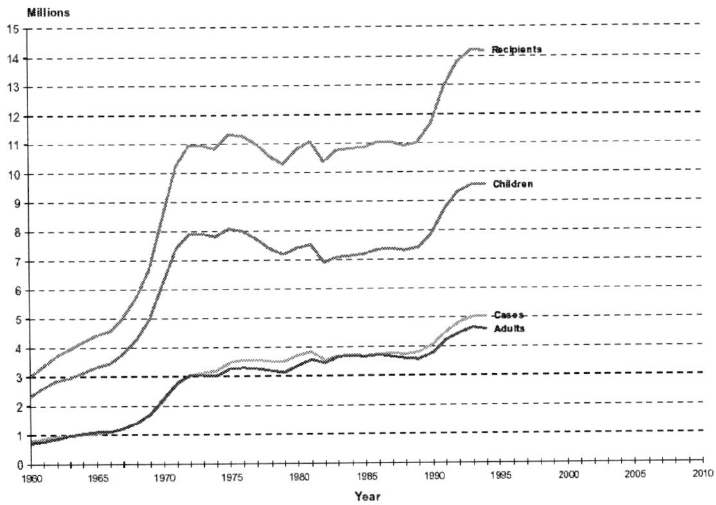

Source: Figure prepared by the Congressional Research Service (CRS) from the Department of Health and Human Services (DHHS), Office of Family Assistance (OFA), available at http://www.acf.hhs.gov/programs/ofa/ data-reports/index.htm. See Table C-2 for supporting data.

Figure 2. Number of Recipients and Cases Receiving Assistance Under AFDC, 1960 to 1994 (Annual monthly average, in millions).

The surge in recipients and cases over the course of the 1960s reflects a variety of factors, including the baby boom generation entering adulthood; an increase in the number and share of children living in female-headed families with a high likelihood of being poor; a rediscovery of poverty in the United States and resultant efforts to address its causes and consequences; and outreach efforts by government and organizations to aid the poor by helping to ensure that they were treated fairly and received benefits to which they were entitled. Additionally, during the late 1960s and early 1970s, U.S. Supreme Court rulings overturned a number of state practices that had denied providing assistance to entitled individuals. Thus, AFDC caseload growth over the period reflected both a growth in the number of persons legally entitled to receive benefits and also an increasing likelihood that legally entitled individuals would be granted benefits. From 1966 to 1971, the number of AFDC recipients would more than double, from 4.5 million to 10.2 million persons. By one estimate, by 1971 90% of families eligible to receive AFDC were participating in the program, compared to only about 33% in the early 1960s.[6] As the AFDC caseload was increasing, Congress began taking action in an attempt to restrict its growth. Among its provisions, amendments to the Social Security Act in 1967 sought to restrict AFDC caseload growth through the establishment of work and training requirements for adult recipients, and an effort to freeze federal matching payments to states with additional caseload growth attributable to cases with an absent parent (i.e., other than widows, or disabled parents). (See Appendix A for brief history of the AFDC program.)

Policy Landscape on the Eve of 1996 Welfare Reform

A variety of welfare reforms were already beginning to be implemented by states in the years preceding the more sweeping reforms that would be allowed under the 1996 welfare reform law. The Family Support Act of 1988 (P.L. 100-485) extended work requirements (which could include work preparation activities such as education and training) for mothers with a child as young as six to mothers with a child as young as three and, at a state's option, extended work requirements to mothers with a child as young as age one. A number of states experimented with changes to welfare policy under waiver authority granted to the Secretary of the Department of Health and

Human Services (DHHS).[7] Among the features of state programs tested under waiver authority were efforts to strengthen work requirements, experiments requiring a "work first" approach rather than "training first, followed by work," time limits, strengthened sanctions for noncompliance with welfare rules, and capping of welfare benefits for a new baby conceived or born while a mother was receiving welfare. In addition, eligibility and funding for child care was expanded, helping to make work possible for mothers who otherwise might have difficulty finding affordable child care. The Family Support Act expanded eligibility for child care assistance in the form of transitional child care assistance for families working their way off AFDC, as well as for families "at risk" of qualifying for AFDC. In 1990, federally funded child care assistance was extended to low-income families generally, not just those receiving or at risk of receiving welfare, under the Child Care and Development Block Grant (CCDBG).

The number of cases and persons receiving AFDC remained relatively level during the 1970s and most of the 1980s, but it began to rise again in 1989 just prior to the onset of an eight-month long economic recession that was marked as beginning in July 1990[8] (see Figure 2, above). From 1988 to 1994, the number of persons receiving AFDC would increase by 30%—a much larger increase than might be expected from the recession alone.[9] The caseload increase contributed to new calls for welfare reform—and welfare reform would once again move into the policy spotlight.

Welfare Dependency as a Political Theme

In his January 1992 State of the Union Address before a joint session of Congress, President G. H. W. Bush, who would be running for a second term as president, expressed his intention to make it quicker and easier for states to restructure their welfare programs through the federal waiver process:

> Welfare was never meant to be a lifestyle. It was never meant to be a habit. It was never supposed to be passed from generation to generation like a legacy. It's time to replace the assumptions of the welfare state and help reform the welfare system.
>
> States throughout the country are beginning to operate with new assumptions that when able-bodied people receive Government assistance, they have responsibilities to the taxpayer: A responsibility to seek work, education, or job training; a responsibility to get their lives in order; a responsibility to hold their families together and refrain from

having children out of wedlock; and a responsibility to obey the law. We are going to help this movement. Often, State reform requires waiving certain Federal regulations. I will act to make that process easier and quicker for every State that asks for our help.[10]

In September 1992, during a presidential campaign speech, candidate William J. Clinton pledged, if elected, to "end welfare as we know it." As reported in the *New York Times*, he stated:

> The changing face of welfare and the changing nature of it, and the enormous barriers of people moving from welfare to a productive life deserve special attention ... Especially now that most people on welfare are young women and their little children.... By the time we're through, we shouldn't have a welfare program in America ... We ought to have a helping hand program followed by a jobs program.[11]

The previous day, the Clinton campaign began airing a campaign ad in which the candidate stated his plan to "end welfare as we know it":

> For so long, Government has failed us, and one of its worst failures has been welfare. I have a plan to end welfare as we know it, to break the cycle of welfare dependency. We'll provide education, job training and child care, but even those who are able must go to work, either in the private sector or in public service.... It's time to make welfare what it should be—a second chance, not a way of life."[12]

Nearly 20 welfare reform bills would be introduced in the 103rd Congress,[13] but it was not until June 1994, before the mid-term elections, that President Clinton would unveil his welfare reform proposal, the Work and Responsibility Act of 1994 (S. 2224, H.R. 4605).

Three months later, House Republicans announced their *Contract with America* just six weeks before the mid-term elections. The document, unveiled on September 27, 1994, included wide-ranging provisions, including changes to House rules, and legislative proposals to address 10 policy domains ranging from fiscal responsibility, crime, national security, and job creation to welfare reform, among others. In the introduction to the welfare reform provisions, the *Contract* viewed the issue as follows:

> Isn't it time for the government to encourage work rather than rewarding dependency? The Great Society has had the unintended consequence of snaring millions of Americans into the welfare trap.

> Government programs designed to give a helping hand to the neediest of Americans have instead bred illegitimacy, crime, illiteracy, and more poverty. Our *Contract with America* will change this destructive social behavior by requiring welfare recipients to take personal responsibility for the decisions they make. Our *Contract* will achieve what some thirty years of massive welfare spending has not been able to accomplish: reduce illegitimacy, require work, and save taxpayers money.[14]

The *Contract's* welfare proposal, the Work Opportunity Act of 1995, was introduced as H.R. 4 on January 4, 1995, the first day of the 104th Congress.

EITC Expansions - "Making Work Pay"

The Earned Income Tax Credit (EITC), first introduced in 1975, was meant to help offset social security (FICA[15]) taxes paid by workers with lower earnings. Since then, the EITC has become an important policy tool in helping to encourage work. Legislated expansions to the credit over the years have increased the size and scope of the credit, extending its reach to higher earned income levels. As a supplement to families with low earnings, the EITC not only helps offset FICA payroll taxes and federal income taxes families would otherwise pay, but it also helps to offset some of the *"implicit taxes"* families face as public assistance benefits are reduced when their income increases. As a *refundable* tax credit, the EITC provides payments to qualified individuals with no federal income tax liability. Over the period examined in this report, the EITC was expanded both under the G.H.W. Bush Administration in 1990 (phased-in in 1991 and 1992), and early in the first term of the Clinton Administration in 1993 (phased-in from 1994 through 1996). By 1996, the expanded EITC was providing a "work bonus" to families with children, amounting to as much as 34 cents on each dollar earned for a low-income family with one child, and as much as 40 cents for a family with two or more. The EITC expansions early in President Clinton's first term were the centerpiece of part of a policy of "making work pay"—that people who work shouldn't be poor—and a critical first step towards the President's campaign promise to "end welfare as we know it" by moving people off public cash assistance and into work.

TANF AND OTHER POLICIES IN THE POST-AFDC ERA

Temporary Assistance for Needy Families (TANF), signed into law in 1996 as part of the Personal Responsibility and Work Opportunity Reconciliation Act (PRWORA, P.L. 104-193), replaced the 61-year-old Aid to Families with Dependent Children (AFDC) program, a federal entitlement program to low-income families with children. TANF eliminated the federal entitlement to assistance that existed under AFDC, replacing an open-ended matching grant program with a fixed-dollar block grant program (with the possible addition of recession-related contingency funds). States must maintain spending levels equal to 75% of what they spent on AFDC at the time the program was repealed—a provision known as State Maintenance of Effort (MOE). Adults must be engaged in approved "work activities" within two years of initial TANF receipt, subject to sanction for noncompliance. Under TANF, federal work participation standards (i.e., "work-requirements") apply to states' TANF caseloads. As such, states are required to have 50% of families, and 90% of two-parent families, engaged in "work" or they will be at risk of having their block grant reduced.[16] TANF gives states increased flexibility to design programs to assist needy families with children compared to its predecessor program, but with fixed federal dollars. A major goal of TANF is to end dependence of needy families on government assistance by limiting the time they may receive assistance and by promoting job preparation, work, and marriage. TANF law imposes a maximum five-year lifetime limit on receipt of federally funded assistance,[17] and allows states to impose shorter limits than the maximum.

States have implemented a wide range of policy options and program approaches in the design of their TANF programs. Many of their programs have evolved from approaches first experimented with under federal waiver authority in the pre-TANF era. Cash welfare under the AFDC program was an entitlement, though states were allowed to set income-eligibility levels and the size of cash benefits, which, under the program, varied widely among them. Since passage of TANF, states' cash welfare programs have evolved over time, becoming more complex and diverging from the cash assistance rules in place under AFDC. States' TANF policies vary widely in determining who is eligible for assistance, the benefits they receive, the behavioral requirements recipients must meet, and the duration they may receive assistance. States' cash welfare policies are described elsewhere.[18] Since the passage of TANF, most states have increased financial work incentives for families receiving cash assistance by allowing families to keep more of their cash welfare benefit as their earnings increase.[19] Additionally, as was the case before welfare reform, most states have allowed inflation to substantially erode the real value of welfare benefits over time, diminishing the value of welfare relative to work.[20]

States may use both federal and state MOE dollars for a wide range of activities, other than the provision of "cash assistance."[21] In FY2009, only 28% of total federal TANF and state (MOE) dollars under the program went toward basic cash assistance. When administrative costs and work activities are added to basic cash assistance—the three spending categories most commonly associated with "welfare"—those expenditures accounted for less than half (42%) of total TANF spending in FY2009. States have also redirected funds previously used to provide cash assistance to pay for child care, either directly or by transferring funds to the child care block grant. In FY2009, 18% of all TANF funds used were either expended on child care or transferred to the Child Care Development Fund (CCDF). TANF is also a major contributor to the child welfare system, which provides foster care, adoption assistance, and services to families with children who either have experienced or are at risk of experiencing child abuse or neglect. It should be noted that among state and federal TANF spending, only those dollars provided as "cash assistance" are included as income for poverty measurement purposes, although dollars expended for other purposes, such as child care, may help to indirectly reduce poverty by making it "affordable" for a parent to work.

Other Federal and State Policies that Encourage Work

In addition to policy changes described above, a variety of other policies implemented at both the federal and state levels have served to reward work. Over the period examined in this report, the minimum wage was increased six times—three times in the pre-welfare reform era and three times since.[22] Moreover, in 29 states state minimum wages exceeded the federal minimum wage in one or more years over the period.[23] Many states have implemented state earned income tax credits (SEITC), which piggyback on the federal EITC. In most cases, states structure their SEITC as a percentage of the federal EITC. In tax year 2000, for example, 14 states and the District of Columbia had SEITCs, and in 10 of those jurisdictions, the credit was fully refundable. By tax year 2010, 23 states and the District of Columbia had SEITCs, and in 19 of those jurisdictions the credit was fully refundable.[24]

Child Support Enforcement[25]

The Child Support Enforcement (CSE) program was enacted in 1975 as a federal-state program (Title IV-D of the Social Security Act). The CSE program is funded with both state and federal dollars. The federal government bears the majority of CSE program expenditures and provides incentive payments to the states for success in meeting CSE program goals.[26]

The CSE program provides seven major services on behalf of children: (1) locating absent parents, (2) establishing paternity, (3) establishing child support orders, (4) reviewing and modifying child support orders, (5) collecting child support payments, (6) distributing child support payments, and (7) establishing and enforcing support for children's medical needs.

The CSE program has the potential to impact more children and for longer periods of time than most other federal programs. In many cases, the CSE program may interact with parents and children for 18 years.

One of the original purposes of the CSE program was to recover from noncustodial parents some of the costs of providing cash welfare to their children's families. Families receiving cash assistance must assign (legally turn-over) to the state their rights to child support collections. These collections are split between the federal government and the states to recover the costs of providing cash assistance. States have options to pay some or all of such collections to families directly, but are not required to do so.

Over the last 10-15 years, the CSE program has expanded its mission beyond its initial welfare cost-recovery goal to focus on providing its clients with more effective and efficient CSE services and fostering parental responsibility. The 1996 welfare reform law established some new systems for tracking down and enforcing the obligations of noncustodial parents to pay child support. It also established a "family first" policy, sending more collected child support on behalf of families that formerly received cash assistance directly to the family. These policy changes, combined with the decline in cash assistance rolls, have resulted in the bulk of CSE collections going directly to families. In FY2010, the CSE program collected $26.6 billion in child support payments from noncustodial parents and served 15.9 million child support cases. Of the $26.5 billion collected in child support payments, about 93% went to families, 6% went to state and federal governments, and 1% consisted of medical support payments or fees paid to states.

Policies Addressing Marriage and Childbearing[27]

Among TANF's four stated goals, three relate directly to marriage and childbearing (*italics added, below*). States may spend TANF funds on a wide range of activities for cash welfare recipients and other families towards achieving these goals.

TANF's Four Goals

1) "Provide assistance to needy families so that children may be cared for in their own homes or in the homes of relatives;
2) end the dependence of needy parents on government benefits by *promoting* job preparation, work, and *marriage*;
3) *prevent and reduce the incidence of out-of-wedlock pregnancies and establish annual numerical goals for preventing and reducing the incidence of these pregnancies*; and
4) *encourage the formation and maintenance of two-parent families*."

Since TANF became law, a number of federal, state, and local initiatives have been undertaken in the attempt to reduce nonmarital childbearing, to promote responsible fatherhood, and healthy marriage. Policy initiatives seek to reduce the incidence of teenage pregnancy, through abstinence education, comprehensive sex education programs, and youth programs. Other programs focus on promoting healthy marriage generally through public advertising campaigns on the value of marriage, and more targeted efforts at providing "social skills" education and training (e.g., marriage education, conflict resolution, and relationship skills,) to couples interested in marriage, or who are already married. Responsible fatherhood programs are intended to connect or reconnect children to their noncustodial parents, with the hope of improving the prospects of children being raised in single parent families.

POLICY RESPONSES TO CHANGING ECONOMIC CONDITIONS

It is useful to view the policy changes discussed above in context of prevailing economic conditions. Over the 23 years examined, the country experienced three economic recessions. The first, lasting 8 months (July 1990 to March 1991), occurring well before welfare reform, was followed by the longest period of economic expansion in the post-World War II era. The expansion ended with a second 8-month long recession (March to November of 2001), well after passage and state implementation of new welfare reform rules. More recently the economy is recovering from the longest and deepest recession in the post-World War II era, having lasted 18 months (from December 2007 to June 2009). The unemployment rate, after having peaked at 10.1% in 2009, has only slowly improved, and is not expected to approach a "natural level" until 2016.[28] Given the depth and duration of the most recent recession, Congress passed a wide range of provisions under economic stimulus and recovery legislation to bolster the economy and to help support low- and middle-income families and individuals.

Tax Rebates and Credits

A number of policy interventions were undertaken in response to the most recent recession, to both stimulate the economy, as well as to cushion the most economically vulnerable. Under provisions in the Economic Stimulus Act of 2008 (P.L. 110-185), single and head-of-household tax filers, such as single mothers, who had filed federal income taxes in 2007 became eligible to receive a minimum tax rebate in 2008 of $300 ($600 for married joint filers) if their 2007 earned income (plus any Social Security benefits, tier 1 railroad retirement, and veteran's disability payments) was at least $3,000, and up to $600 ($1,200 for married joint filers) to the extent of their 2008 tax liability. The American Recovery and Reinvestment Act (ARRA) (P.L. 111-5) provided rebates of up to $400 for single and head-of-household tax filers, and up to $800 for joint filers, in 2009, by reducing FICA tax withholding.

The Emergency and Economic Stabilization Act of 2008 (EESA) (P.L. 110-343) included a provision that temporarily lowered the income limit for receipt of the refundable portion of the Child Tax Credit[29] (CTC), which is administered by the Internal Revenue Service (IRS) as the Additional Child Tax Credit (ACTC), to distinguish it from the nonrefundable portion of the CTC. Refundable credits, such as the ACTC and EITC, extend benefits to tax filers even though they owe no taxes. For the 2008 tax year, EESA effectively lowered the ACTC refundable income limit from $12,050, to $8,500. ARRA further temporarily expanded eligibility for the ACTC to tax filers with earnings of $3,000 or more for tax years 2009 and 2010. The refundable income limits set a lower threshold at which tax filers may begin to receive the refundable ACTC. A tax filer with a qualifying child could receive a "refund" amounting to 15 cents on every dollar earned above the refundable income threshold, up to a maximum credit amount of $1,000 per qualifying child. Under the EESA, a single mother with earned income of $12,050 became eligible for an ACTC of $532.50 in 2008, whereas absent the EESA provisions she would have received nothing. In 2009, under the ARRA provisions, a single parent with one child and having annual earnings in excess over $3,000 may be eligible for the credit, and eligible for the full $1,000 credit once her earned income reaches $9,667.[30] Absent the legislative changes noted above, she would not have begun to become eligible for the credit until her earned income exceeded $12,550, and would not have been eligible for the full $1,000 credit until her income reached $19,217.[31]

Under ARRA certain ACTC provisions were set to expire at the end of the 2010 tax year. Among other things, expiring provisions would have caused the maximum allowable credit to revert from $1,000 to $500 per qualifying child, and for credit refundability to extend only to families with three or more qualifying children. The Tax Relief, Unemployment Insurance Reauthorization, and Job Creation Act of 2010 (P.L. 111-312) extends the ARRA ACTC provisions through tax year 2012.

ARRA also temporarily raised the EITC credit rate for tax years 2009 and 2010 from 40% for families with *two or more* qualifying children to 45% for families with *three or more* qualifying children. In 2009, for a single parent with three or more children, the maximum available credit under ARRA increased to $5,657, from what otherwise would have been $5,028 absent ARRA. The Tax Relief, Unemployment Insurance Reauthorization, and Job Creation Act of 2010 (P.L. 111-312) extended the ARRA EITC provisions through tax year 2012.

Unemployment Insurance Benefits

Unemployment Compensation (UC) under the Unemployment Insurance (UI) system typically provides up to 26 weeks of unemployment compensation covering a portion of lost wages to qualified covered workers who become eligible due to job loss.[32] Under the permanent Extended Benefits (EB) program, unemployment compensation may be extended for an additional 13 or 20 weeks to workers in qualifying states with high unemployment. Both UC and EB payments to workers are funded jointly through federal and state taxes on employers. Additionally, as in some past recessions, Congress funded a temporary Emergency Unemployment Compensation program (EUC08, P.L. 110-252), which began in 2008.[33] Under the EB and EUC08 programs, Unemployment Insurance (UI) benefits have been extended from a maximum 26 weeks under the UC program, up to a maximum of 60 to 99 weeks, depending on states' circumstances.

Additionally, ARRA made several changes to Unemployment Compensation (UC) to assist individuals who become unemployed.[34] It provided a temporary supplemental benefit increase of $25 per week under all UC programs (UC, EB, EUC08, and others[35]), payable until July 2010, and excluded $2,400 in UC benefits from gross income under the federal income tax for 2009. ARRA also provided $7 billion in incentives to states to modify their basis for computing UC benefits and for extending benefits to currently ineligible individuals. Two-thirds of the $7 billion available to states is contingent on states first adopting an alternative method of determining eligibility for individuals who do not qualify under the regular method, based on their wage and employment history. The states could then be eligible for the remaining two-thirds of the $7 billion if they adopt at least two of the following four provisions:

1. permit former part-time workers to seek part-time work;
2. permit voluntary separations from employment for compelling family reasons, which must include (i) domestic violence, (ii) illness or disability of an immediate family member, and (iii) the need to accompany a spouse who is relocating for employment;
3. provide extended compensation to UC recipients in qualifying training programs for high demand occupations; or
4. provide dependents' allowances to UC recipients with dependents.

Upon accepting the federal incentive payments, states are required to maintain the adopted changes after the incentive payments expire. The above provisions could especially assist single mothers who whose job attachment has been sporadic or limited to part-time employment due to competing family responsibilities.

Supplemental Nutrition Assistance Program (SNAP/Food Stamp) Benefits

ARRA raised maximum benefit amounts under the Supplemental Nutrition Assistance Program (SNAP, formerly the Food Stamp program), effective in April 2009.[36] ARRA effectively increased maximum monthly SNAP benefits by 13.6%, as a replacement for annual benefit adjustments based on annual food-price inflation. As a result, *average* household benefits (typically less than the maximum) were boosted by more than 15%. Under current funding levels, ARRA SNAP benefit increases are projected to be maintained until October 31, 2013, at which time SNAP benefit adjustments will revert back to annual adjustment based on food-price inflation, as specified in SNAP law.

Other Social Policies

ARRA also included provisions that added a new temporary "emergency contingency fund" under TANF for FY2009 and FY2010, which allowed states receiving extra federal grants to cover 80% of increased recession-related costs in those two years.[37] Recession-related costs are defined as increased basic assistance (for states with increased basic assistance caseloads), nonrecurrent short-term benefits, or subsidized employment expenditures.

Other ARRA provisions may also directly help single mothers.[38] For example, expanded funding for child care for low-income working families might help single mothers secure and retain employment, and increased federal incentive payments to states to run effective child support enforcement programs may help states' efforts to establish and maintain absent parents' child support obligations.

WELFARE, WORK, AND POVERTY STATUS OF FEMALE-HEADED FAMILIES WITH CHILDREN

A dramatic transformation in single mothers' welfare, work, and poverty status has occurred over the 23-year period examined in this report. The period has seen a marked *structural change* in the provision of benefits under a number of programs that contribute to the fabric of the nation's "income safety net." In turn, single mothers' *behavior has changed* markedly over the period, in part response to structural changes to income "safety net" programs, with more mothers working, and fewer relying on cash welfare to support themselves and their children in the post welfare reform era, than before.

Figure 3 completes the administrative data series presented earlier (Figure 2) through 2010. The figure shows a dramatic decline in the number of recipients (total, adults and children) receiving AFDC/TANF after having reached an historic peak in 1993. In 1993, 14.2 million persons were receiving ADFC in the average month; by 2008, the number receiving TANF had fallen to 4 million, a decline of 10.2 million persons from 2003, comprised of 6.5 million fewer children and 3.7 million fewer adults. In 2008, the number of persons receiving cash aid under TANF was the lowest since 1963, when 3.9 million received assistance under AFDC. Reflecting the effects of the most recent recession, the number of persons receiving TANF has increased from 4.0 million in 2008, to 4.6 million in 2010.

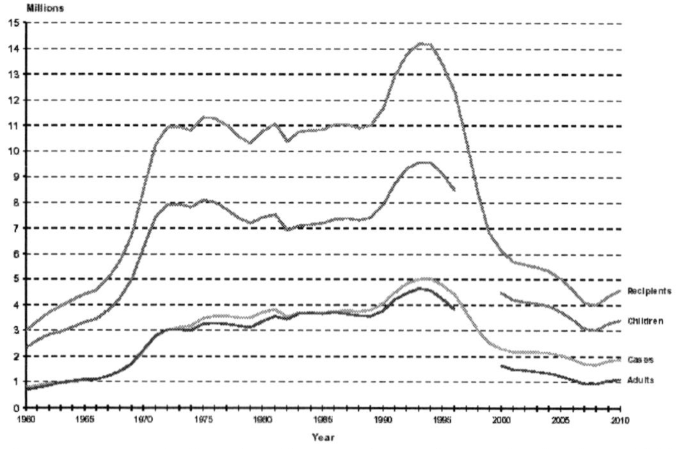

Source: Figure prepared by the Congressional Research Service (CRS) from Department of Health and Human Services (DHHS), Office of Family Assistance (OFA), available at http://www.acf.hhs.gov/programs/ofa/data-reports/index.htm. See Table C-2 for supporting data.

Note: Separate estimates for children and adults are not available from 1997 to 1999 due to changes in state reporting requirements during the transition from AFDC to TANF.

Figure 3. Number of Recipients and Cases Receiving Assistance Under ADC, AFDC, and TANF, 1960 to 2010 (Annual Monthly Average, in Millions).

Moreover, since welfare reform, poverty among children living in female-headed households[39] has also fallen significantly. Figure 4 shows that the incidence of poverty among children in female-headed households fell from 55.4% in 1991, to 39.3% by 2001, representing the largest ten-year decline in poverty among such children since that which commenced in the early 1960s. The poverty rate of children in female-headed families has risen consequent to two recessions since 2001, reaching a recent high of 44.4% in 2009. Since 1996 welfare reform, progress appears to have been largely sustained in both reducing welfare dependency and poverty among children in female-headed families, in spite of the recent recession.

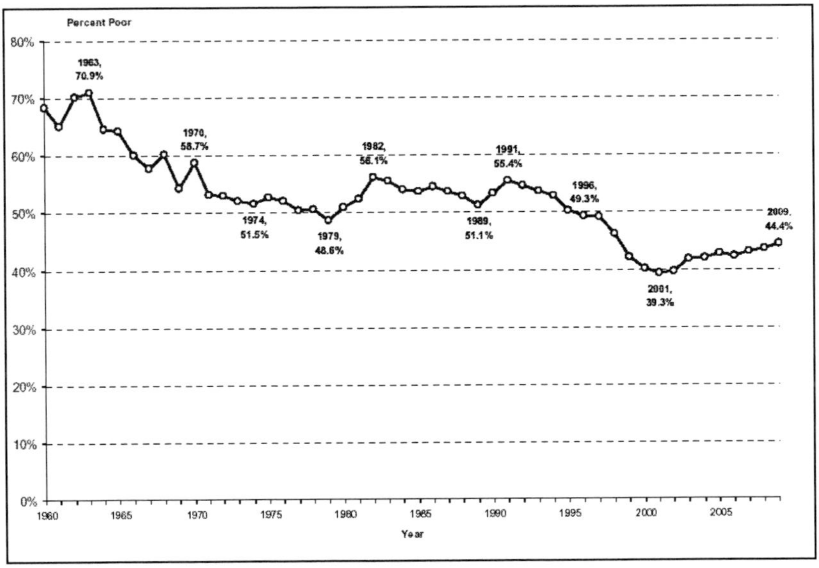

Source: Figure prepared by the Congressional Research Service (CRS) based on U.S. Census Bureau historical series, available at http://www.census.gov/hhes/www/poverty/data/historical/people.html, "Table 10. Related Children in Female Householder Families, by Poverty Status." See Table C-3 for supporting data.

Notes: Estimates are for children in female-headed "households," which differs somewhat from the CRS definition of female-headed "families" used later in this report based on analysis of U.S. Census Bureau Current Population Survey (CPS) Annual Social and Economic Supplement (ASEC) data.

Figure 4. Poverty Rate of Children Under Age 18 in Female-Headed Households (No Spouse Present), 1960 to 2009 (Percent poor).

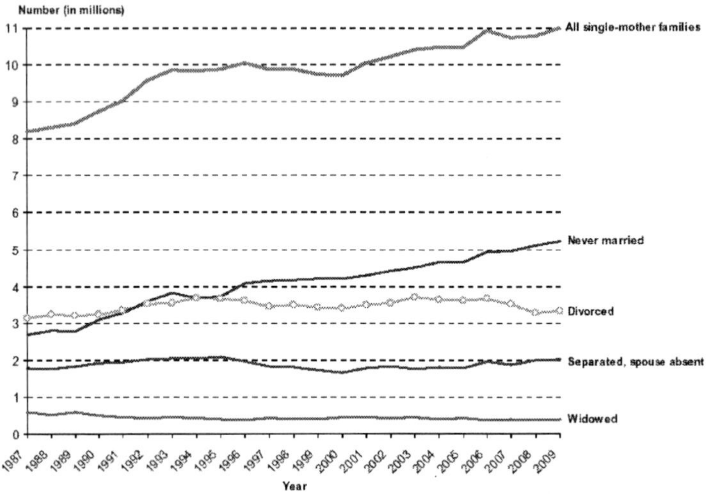

Source: Prepared by the Congressional Research Service (CRS) based on analysis of U.S. Census Bureau 1988 to 2010 Current Population Survey (CPS) Annual Social and Economic Supplement (ASEC) data. See Table C-4 for supporting data.

Figure 5. Number of Single-Mother Families, by Mothers' Marital Status, 1987 to 2009 (Number in millions).

The remainder of this report focuses primarily on single mothers, as single mothers have been a primary focus of social policy. Untangling the effects of demographic factors, the economy, welfare policy and other policy interventions on single mothers' work behavior, welfare receipt, income, and poverty status, is beyond the scope of this report. Others have attempted to parcel out these effects with mixed success and differing conclusions as to the relative impacts of each.[40] In contrast to these efforts, the remainder of this report provides a descriptive analysis of U.S. Census Bureau CPS/ASEC data, with the goal of increasing understanding of changes in single mothers' welfare, work, income and poverty status that have occurred over the past 23 years.

Number of Families Headed by Single Mothers

Over the 23-year period examined, the number of single-mother families increased from 8.2 million in 1987 to 11.0 million in 2009 (Figure 5). The total number of single mothers increased from 8.4 million in 1989 to about 9.9 million in 1993, an increase of 1.5 million, or 17%. From 1993 through 2000, the number of single mothers remained fairly stable, ranging between 9.7 million and 10.1 million. Since 2000, the number of single mothers has increased by 1.3 million, from 9.7 million in 2000 to 11.0 million in 2009. The overall increase in single-mother families has largely been due to an increase in single mothers who have never been married. From 1987 to 2009, the number of never-married single mothers increased from 2.7 million to 5.2 million, an increase of 2.5 million, or 94%, over the period. In contrast, the number of separated mothers (no spouse present) increased by 232,000, a 13% increase, and the number of divorced mothers increased by 203,000, a 6% increase; the number of widowed mothers fell by 175,000, a 30% decrease. In contrast, the number of married-couple families with children increased by 406,000, a 2% increase, over the period (not shown in the figure).

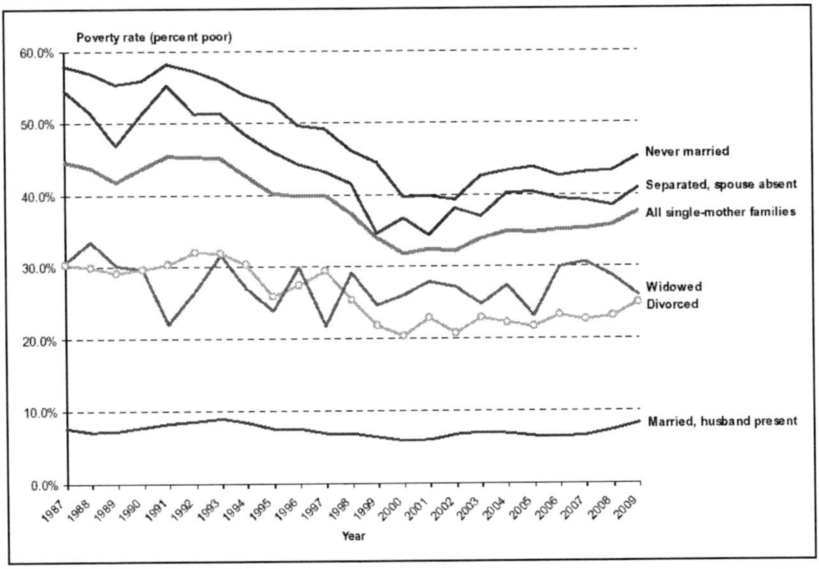

Source: Prepared by the Congressional Research Service (CRS) based on analysis of U.S. Census Bureau 1988 to 2010 Current Population Survey (CPS) Annual Social and Economic Supplement (ASEC) data. See Table C-4 for supporting data.

Figure 6. Poverty Rates by Mothers' Marital Status, 1987 to 2009 (Percent poor).

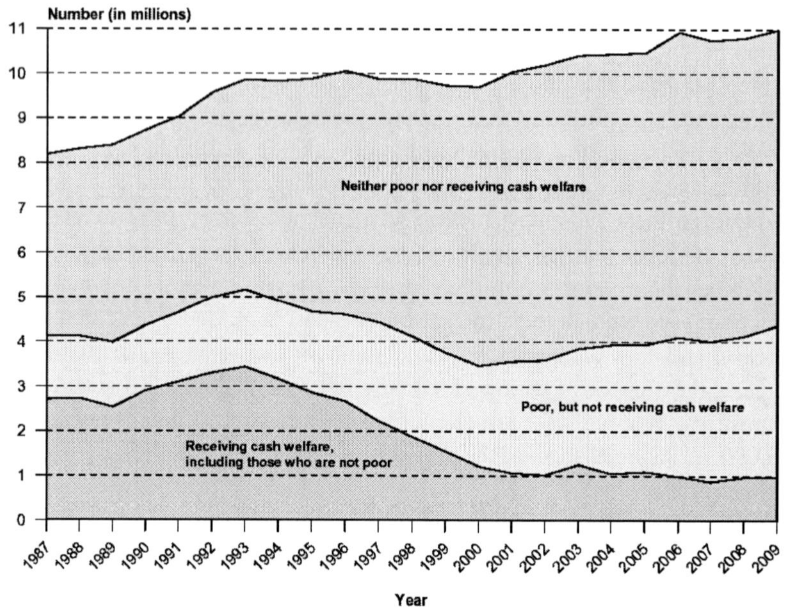

Source: Prepared by the Congressional Research Service (CRS) based on analysis of U.S. Census Bureau 1988 to 2010 Current Population Survey (CPS) Annual Social and Economic Supplement (ASEC) data. See Table C-5 for supporting data.

Note: Welfare is cash welfare in the form of AFDC, TANF, or state General Assistance.

Figure 7. Single Mothers: Poverty and Cash Welfare Receipt, 1987 to 2009.

Incidence of Poverty by Mothers' Marital Status

The incidence of poverty among families headed by single mothers fell substantially from a peak of 45.4% of all single-mother families in 1992 and 1993 to an historic low for the 23-year period of 31.8% in 2000 (Figure 6). Since 2000, poverty rates for single mothers have increased, but still remain well below levels of the early 1990s. The poverty rate among single-mother families rose to 34.9% by 2004, consequent to an 8 month-long recession (March to November 2001 and continued to drift upwards, until more sharply increasing, to 37.6% in 2009, consequent to a deep 18 month-long recession (December 2007 to June 2009). Poverty rates are highest among never-married mothers, followed by separated mothers (no spouse present) and widowed and divorced mothers. Poverty rates of single mothers are several times that of married mothers. Poverty rates for never-married, separated, and divorced mothers fell substantially over the 1990s, reaching historic lows by the beginning of the next decade. (Note: the wide variability in the poverty rate among widowed mothers over the period reflects sample variation relating to the comparatively small sample of such mothers represented on the CPS/ASEC.)

Poverty and Cash Welfare Receipt among Single Mothers

CPS data show an increase in cash welfare receipt (AFDC, TANF, or General Assistance (GA)[41]) among single mothers during the late 1980s and early 1990s and a decrease in the mid- to late-1990s. The CPS data generally correspond to the caseload rise and fall documented by administrative program data, but underestimate the caseload statistics to some extent.[42] Figure 7 shows that the number of single mothers in families reporting receipt of cash welfare on the CPS increased from 2.5 million in 1989 to 3.4 million in 1993, an increase of 900,000, or 36%, over the four-year period. Compared to 1993, the peak year of welfare receipt, the number of single mothers reporting cash welfare was down to under 1 million (967,000) in 2009—a 72% decline from 1993 (the bottom-shaded portion of the figure).[43] The CPS/ASEC data show very little if any take-up in receipt of cash welfare by single mothers in response to the most recent recession, and little if any take-up in cash welfare in response to the one preceding it. This differs from the administrative data presented earlier (Figure 3) which showed a modest increase in the TANF caseload from 2008 to 2009. From 1993 to 2009, the number of *poor* single mothers who reported *receiving no cash welfare* increased from 1.722 million in 1993 to 3.408 million in 2009, nearly doubling over the period (the middle-shaded area of the figure).

Work, Poverty, and Cash Welfare Receipt of Single Mothers

Figure 8 provides an overview of single mothers' welfare, work and poverty status from 1987 to 2009. The figure shows that since 1993, the share of single mothers who worked at some time during the year has increased markedly and that the share who received cash welfare (AFDC, TANF, or GA) has declined significantly, as has the share who are poor under the official poverty definition. The figure illustrates that while both cash welfare recipiency rates and poverty rates for single mothers have generally fallen since 1993, single mothers' welfare recipiency rate has fallen faster than their poverty rate. More recently, since 2000, the poverty rate of single mothers has increased, but cash welfare receipt has not—a growing share of single mothers are poor under the official poverty measure, but receive no cash welfare assistance. This suggests that TANF and other policies implemented in the mid-1990s (e.g., EITC expansion) may have had a lasting behavioral impact on reducing the incidence of cash welfare receipt among families headed by single mothers.

SINGLE MOTHERS' EMPLOYMENT

While welfare receipt has declined, dramatic gains in single mothers' employment have occurred since 1993. Figure 9 shows employment rates of single and married mothers by age of youngest child in March, from 1988 to 2010. The chart shows that gaps that had existed between single and married mothers' employment have been virtually eliminated in recent years, with single mothers now being as, and in some cases more, likely than their married counterparts to be working.

Over the period, the increase in employment among single mothers with young children has been most dramatic. Among mothers with a child under the age of 3, their employment rate increased from a recent low of 35.1% in March 1993 to a high of 59.1% in March 2000, a 24 percentage point increase over the period. Their employment rate fell to 53.7% in March 2005 but rebounded to 57.0% in March 2006, marking a recent high; it has since fallen, to 52.9% in March 2009. Single mothers with a youngest child aged 3-5 also experienced marked employment gains over the mid-to-late 1990s. Their employment rate grew from a recent low of 54.1% in March 1992, to 72.7% by March 2000, an 18.6 percentage point increase over the period. In March 2008, their employment rate stood at 68.5%, but by March 2010 had fallen to 59.7%—13 percentage points below its March 2000 peak, with over two-thirds of the decline having occurred since March 2007. Single mothers whose youngest child was of school age (age 6-17) had employment rates about equal to those of their married counterparts over the 1988-2010 period. In March 2010, the employment rate of single mothers with school age children stood at 70.7%—8.4 percentage points below a peak employment rate of 79.1% in 2001.

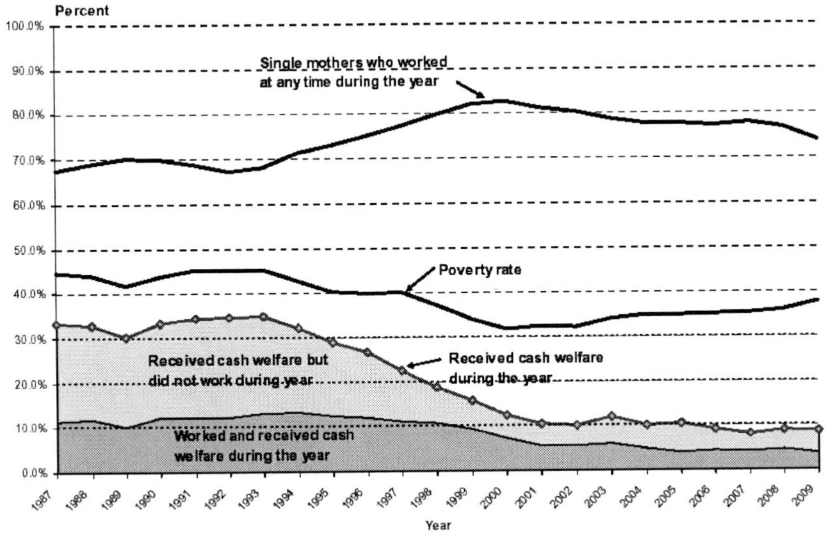

Source: Prepared by the Congressional Research Service (CRS) based on analysis of U.S. Census Bureau 1988 to 2010 Current Population Survey (CPS) Annual Social and Economic Supplement (ASEC) data. See Table C-6 for supporting data.

Note: Welfare is cash welfare in the form of AFDC, TANF, or state General Assistance.

Figure 8. Welfare, Work, and Poverty Status Among Single Mothers, 1987 to 2009.

Unemployment Rates Across the Business Cycle

Based on Bureau of Labor Statistics (BLS) data, the unemployment rate of women maintaining families has increased from a recent low of 6.2% in August 2007, just prior to the recession's onset, to 11.7% in June 2009, the recession's official end-date (see Figure 10). Over a year past the recession's end, the unemployment rate of women maintaining families rose further, to a most recent high of 13.4% in July and August 2010. The annual average unemployment rate among women maintaining families increased from 6.5% in 2007, to 8.0% in 2008, 11.5% in 2009, and to 12.3% in 2010. Whereas poverty estimates for 2010 won't be available until the fall of 2011, persistently high unemployment rates among women maintaining families in 2010 suggest that the incidence of "official" poverty among single mothers and their children in 2010 may eclipse that experienced in 2009. Given the pace of economic recovery, poverty among single mothers and their children may remain above pre-recession levels for some years to come.

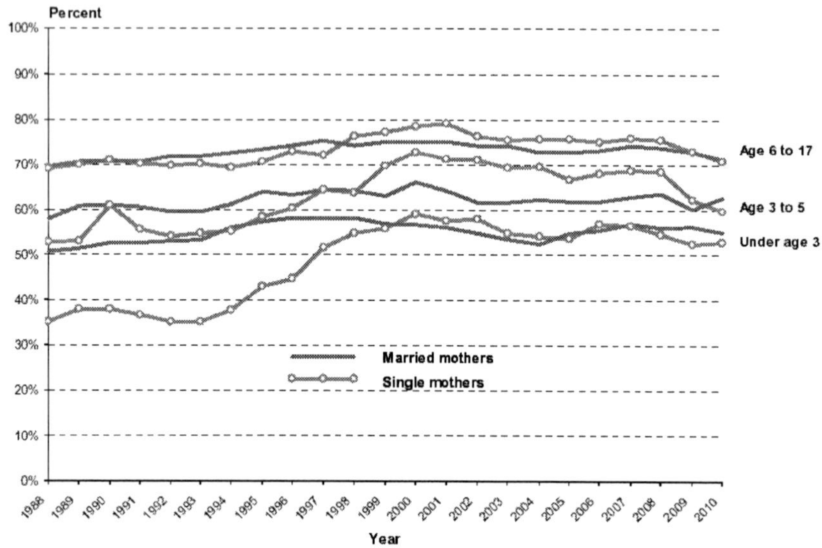

Source: Prepared by the Congressional Research Service (CRS) based on analysis of U.S. Census Bureau 1988 to 2010 Current Population Survey (CPS) Annual Social and Economic Supplement (ASEC) data. See Table C-7 for supporting data.

Figure 9. Employment Rates of Single and Married Mothers, by Age of Youngest Child, March 1988 to March 2010.

Poor Single Mothers' Work and Welfare Status

There is a greater likelihood today than in years past that a *poor* single mother will be working, rather than receiving welfare. Changes in poor mothers' participation in work and welfare status first became evident in the early-to-mid 1990s, with rates of employment increasing after 1992 (solid green line, Figure 11) and rates of welfare receipt declining after 1993 (solid orange line, Figure 11). A crossover point was reached by 1996, when the chances that a poor single mother would be working exceeded the chances that she would be receiving welfare. The initial decline in welfare receipt, and increase in work among poor single mothers coincides with an economy recovering from recession, a phasing in of expanded EITC benefits that encouraged work (1994 – 1996), increased experimentation among states attempting to transform their cash welfare programs through the section 1115 waiver process, and increased political messaging that national welfare was looming on the horizon. The trend of declining welfare receipt and increased work intensified further, after passage of national welfare reform legislation in 1996.

Figure 11 shows that the share of poor single mothers who received cash welfare at any time during the year fell from just over 60% in the 1987-1993 period, to 17% in 2007 and 2009.

Welfare receipt among poor single mothers began to decline significantly after 1993, and even more so after 1996. Similarly, the share of poor single mothers who were working at any time during the year increased from around 44% in 1992, to a peak of 64% in 1999, but has dropped since, to 52% in 2009.

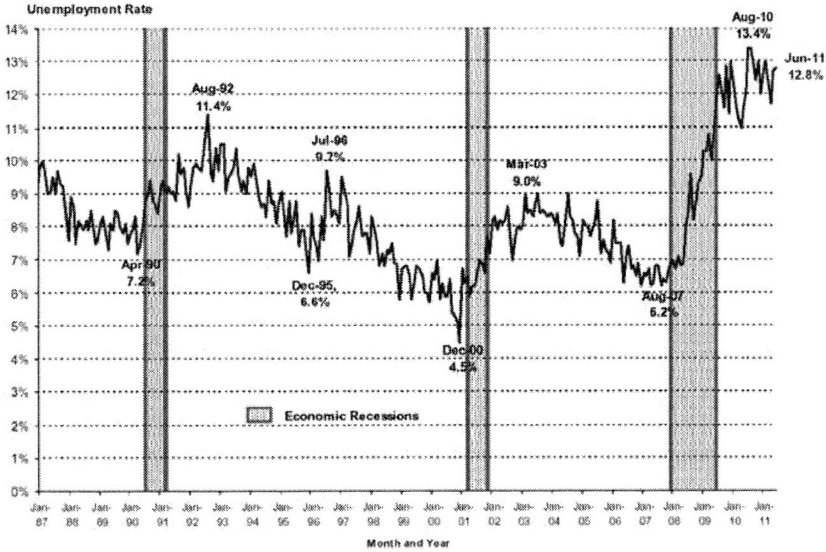

Source: Prepared by the Congressional Research Service (CRS) based on U.S. Bureau of Labor Statistics (BLS) data. See Table C-8 for supporting data.

Notes: Economic recessions: July 1990 to March 1991, March to November 2001, and December 2007 to June 2009. Economic recessions are defined by the National Bureau of Economic Research (NBER) Business Cycle Dating Committee.

Figure 10. Unemployment Rate of Women Maintaining Families, January 1987 through June 2011 (Rates not seasonally adjusted).

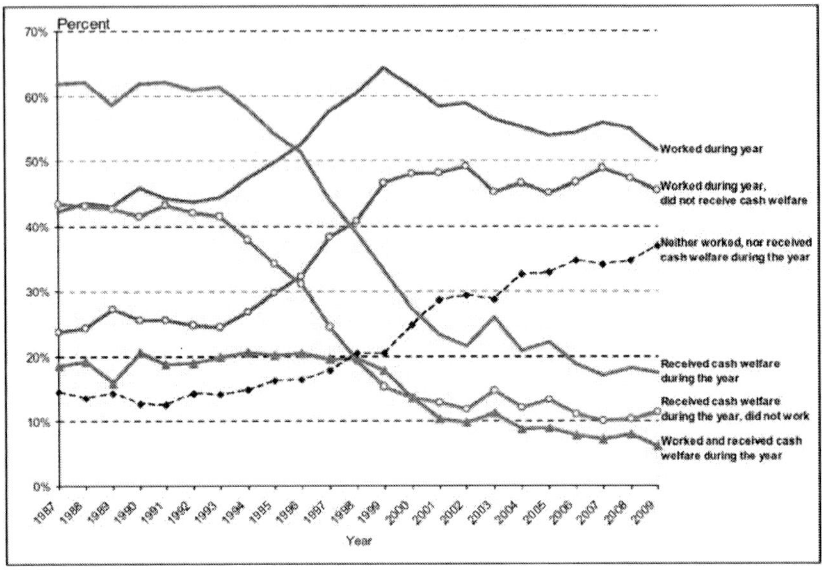

Source: Prepared by the Congressional Research Service (CRS) based on analysis of U.S. Census Bureau 1988 to 2010 Current Population Survey (CPS) Annual Social and Economic Supplement (ASEC) data. See Table C-9 for supporting data.

Figure 11. Poor Single Mothers: Work and Welfare Status During the Year, 1987 to 2009.

The share of poor single mothers who relied on cash welfare without working dropped from a peak of 43% in 1991, to a low of 10% in 2007 (a 77% drop from the 1991 rate). The share who worked without relying on cash welfare has increased from a recent low of nearly 25% in 1993, to 46% in 2009. Poor single mothers who combined work and welfare over the year has fallen by well over two-thirds from 1996 (20%) to 2009 (6%).

Poor single mothers who reported that they neither worked nor received cash welfare during the year (the dashed blue line in Figure 11) has increased from a low of about 12% in 1991 to 37% in 2009. This surprising combination may reflect a mix of circumstances, including income support from unrelated household members (which is not included in the official poverty measure), including cohabiting partners, and other means of support from outside the household not captured on the CPS. It may also reflect income reporting problems on the CPS, especially with regard to welfare income.[44]

RECEIPT OF SELECTED BENEFITS BY "EARNINGS POOR" FEMALE-HEADED FAMILIES WITH CHILDREN

As shown above, cash welfare receipt among female-headed families with children has dramatically declined in the post-1996 welfare reform era, with the decline having begun in the years just prior to the passage and subsequent implementation of reform. Figure 12 shows recipiency rates among female-headed families with children with *earnings* below their families' poverty thresholds, for six income "safety-net" program categories: AFDC, TANF or General Assistance (GA); Supplemental Security Income (SSI); Unemployment Insurance Benefits; Food Stamp/SNAP benefits; the EITC; and the refundable portion of the Child Tax Credit, the Additional Child Tax Credit (ACTC). The analysis is restricted to *"earnings poor"* families, as earnings are the primary means by which most families with working age members support themselves. Earnings (along with other income) deemed insufficient to provide for a family's basic needs (i.e., poverty level income) and the reasons associated with insufficient earnings (or other income) are often used in determining eligibility for need-tested and other programs.

Over the 23-year period examined, there has been a marked change in the provision of benefits among the six programs, reflecting a structural change in aspects of the "income safety net." It is important to note that the "official" U.S. poverty measure does not include in-kind benefits, such as Food Stamp/SNAP benefits, nor does it include tax transfers, in the form of the EITC, or ACTC. Among the six program categories examined, only AFDC/TANF/GA, SSI, and UI are included in the "official" poverty measure. As will be shown later, this has important implications as to how one assesses the role of income support policies, especially in the post 1996 welfare reform era and over the course of the most recent recession and recovery.

Earned Income Tax Credit (EITC)

Figure 12 shows a substantial increase in EITC from 1993 to 1999, as mothers with comparatively low earnings prospects turned away from cash public assistance towards work. In 1993, about 44% of "earnings poor" female-headed families with children are estimated to have received the EITC, by 1999, 64% of such families were estimated to have received it. In contrast, over the same period, cash welfare receipt in the form of AFDC, TANF, or

GA fell from about 56% to 31%. EITC benefit increases that phased in between 1993 and 1996 may have served to lure some single mothers away from welfare, in part evidenced by increased work seen earlier in Figure 9. Additionally, states' use of AFDC waivers to strengthen work requirements and sanctions for noncompliance in the pre-welfare reform years, may have served to increase work participation and consequent EITC receipt. TANF's provisions further encouraged work and accompanying EITC eligibility over welfare. *The figure shows a marked decrease in estimated EITC receipt in 2003 and 2004, and then a rebound in 2005—these years are marked by a dashed-line, as caution should be exercised in attempting to interpret this phenomena, as it appears to be an aberation that is not readily explainable.*[45]

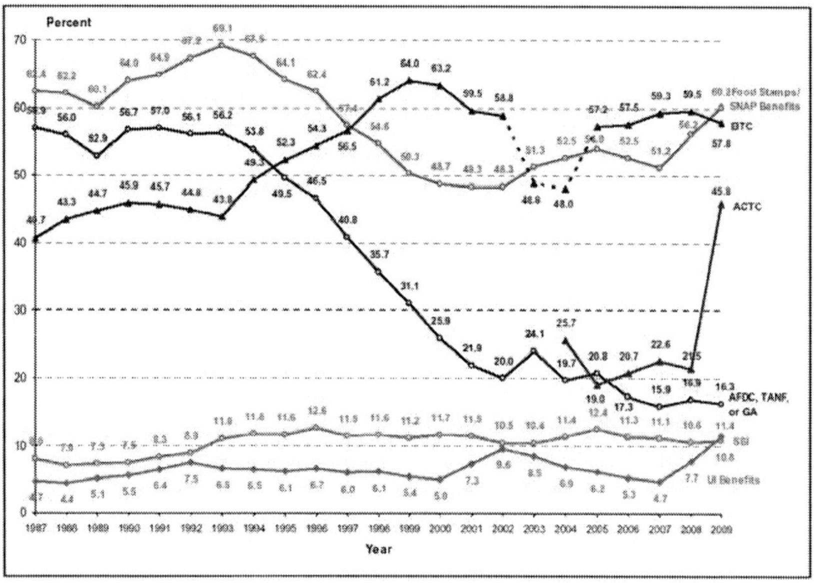

Source: Prepared by the Congressional Research Service (CRS) based on analysis of U.S. Census Bureau 1988 to 2010 Current Population Survey (CPS) Annual Social and Economic Supplement (ASEC) data. See Table C-10 for supporting data.

Notes: "Earnings poor" families are those whose annual earned income is below their poverty income threshold. Other sources of income received by these families might subsequently lift their total income above poverty.

Figure 12. Receipt of Selected Benefits by "Earnings Poor" Female-Headed Families with Children, 1987 to 2009.

Supplemental Security Income (SSI)

Receipt of SSI among families headed by single mothers increased over the first half of the 1990s, as shown in Figure 12. In 1988, 7% of families headed by single mothers reported receiving SSI; by 1996, 12.6% of such families were reporting SSI receipt. The populations served by AFDC and SSI overlap somewhat. Some persons may be eligible for both programs, but individuals cannot receive benefits under both, although families can.[46] In contrast to AFDC and TANF, individuals applying for SSI must pass an often strict and lengthy disability determination process in order to qualify. SSI benefits are higher than those available under AFDC and TANF. Additionally, SSI benefits are fully federally funded, though some states provide supplementary benefits on top of the federal SSI benefit. In contrast, AFDC benefits were jointly funded by states and the federal government, through federal matching dollars, and under TANF through a fixed-dollar federal block grant. As such, if all other things were equal, both individuals and states would do better financially by shifting persons potentially eligible for TANF to SSI, assuming the person was unlikely able to become gainfully employed. Several administrative changes to SSI made it easier for children to be ruled eligible for the program during the early 1990s,[47] which could have contributed to increased SSI receipt among families, including those headed by single mothers.

Unemployment Insurance (UI) Benefits

Receipt of Unemployment Insurance (UI) benefits among families headed by earnings poor single mothers has risen concurrent and consequent to the three economic recessions that occurred over the 23-year period examined (Figure 12). With each recession, UI receipt among these families has increased over that of the previous recession. For example, in the aftermath of the 1990-1991 recession, 7.5% of all earnings poor single mother families reported UI receipt in 1992; following the 2000 recession, 9.6% reported UI receipt 2002; and in the most recent recession, 11.4% reported UI receipt. The higher incidence of UI receipt in 2002 than in 1992 most probably reflects a higher incidence of UI eligibility in the more recent period, due to increased employment of single mothers, as the two recessions were of equal length, and the unemployment rate among women maintaining families was slightly lower in 2002 than in 1992 (see Figure 10, shown earlier). The higher incidence of

UI receipt in 2009 most likely reflects both the severity of the recession, as well as increased UI coverage among single mothers as a result of having better established work histories than in previous years.

Food Stamp/Supplemental Nutrition Assistance Program (SNAP) Benefits

Food Stamp/SNAP benefit receipt is depicted by the green line in Figure 12. The figure shows that Food Stamp/SNAP receipt reached an historic peak among earnings poor single mother families in 1993 (69.3%), subsequent to the 1990-1991 recession. Food Stamp receipt for this group of families reached an historic low in 2002, with 48.3% reporting benefit receipt. The comparatively low rate of Food Stamp receipt in 2002, compared to earlier periods, may in part be attributable to the decline of such families on AFDC/TANF, as persons who enrolled in those programs were generally enrolled in Food Stamps automatically through administrative processes. The figure shows a modest rise in Food Stamp receipt from 2002 to 2005, subsequent to the 2000 recession, and a more substantial rise from 2007 to 2009, consequent to the most recent recession. Still, the SNAP benefit receipt rate among the depicted families in 2009 (60.2%) was nearly identical to that of Food Stamps in 1989, even though economic conditions in 2009 were much worse.

Additional Child Tax Credit (ACTC)

Finally, the figure shows estimated receipt of the Additional Child Tax Credit (ACTC) among depicted families.[48] Census Bureau estimates of ACTC receipt on the CPS are first available beginning in 2004. As discussed earlier ("Tax Rebates and Credits"), the Emergency and Economic Stabilization Act of 2008 (EESA) (P.L. 110-343), temporarily lowered the income threshold for receipt of the ACTC in tax year 2008. There appears to be no discernable effect of the provision from 2007 to 2008 in the CPS/ASEC estimates for depicted families. However, the figure shows that estimated ACTC receipt more than doubled from 2008 (21.5%) to 2009 (45.8%). This large increase in ACTC eligibility reflects changes in The American Recovery and Reinvestment Act (ARRA) (P.L. 111-5) which lowered the ACTC income threshold to $3,000, and took effect in 2009.

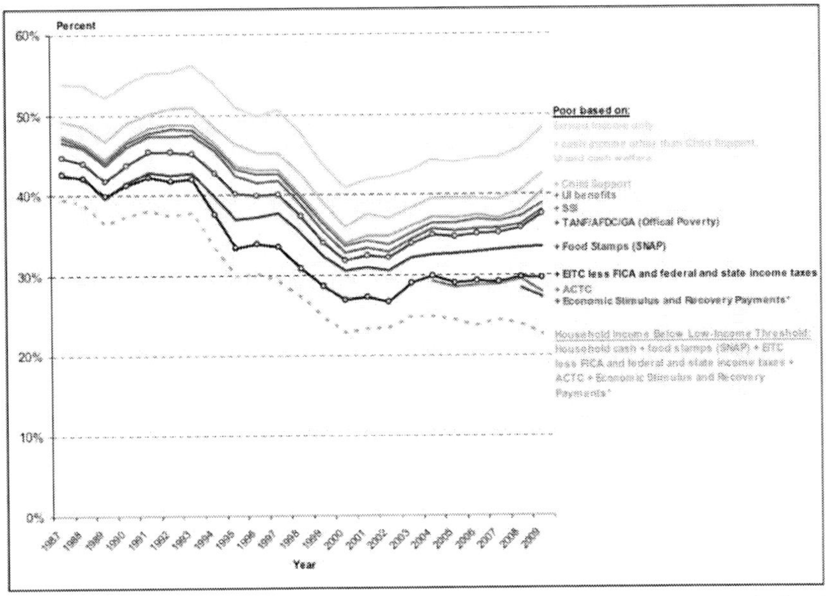

Source: Prepared by the Congressional Research Service (CRS) based on analysis of U.S. Census Bureau 1988 to 2010 Current Population Survey (CPS) Annual Social and Economic Supplement (ASEC) data. See Table C-10 for supporting data.

* Census Bureau estimates of Economic Stimulus Payments received in 2008 and Economic Recovery Payments received in 2009.

Figure 13. Effects of Earnings, Transfers, and Taxes on Family Poverty and Household Low-Income Status of Single Mothers, 1987 to 2009.

EFFECTS OF EARNINGS, TRANSFERS, AND TAXES ON SINGLE MOTHERS' POVERTY STATUS

As shown earlier in Figure 6, single mothers' poverty status has improved since 1993. Changes in the economy and changes in welfare policy and other programs, such as the EITC, have both direct and indirect effects on income and poverty. However, the official U.S. poverty measure counts only family pre-tax cash income (excluding capital gains and lump sum or one-time payments) against families' poverty thresholds (which vary by family size and composition) to determine whether a family is counted as poor. The "official" U.S. poverty definition does not include the value of in-kind benefits, such as

Food Stamp/SNAP benefits, or public housing subsidies, nor does it include the effects of taxes or tax credits such as the EITC and the ACTC. Inclusion of in-kind benefits and refundable tax credits, net of taxes families pay, provides a more comprehensive income definition than the official poverty income definition. Failing to include them can have important implications as to how one assesses the role of income support policies, especially in the post 1996 welfare reform era, and over the course of the most recent recession and recovery. Additionally, other unrelated household members may contribute to the family's economic well-being, but determining the extent to which resources are shared among unrelated household members is difficult.

Figure 13 shows the marginal effects of income from a number of sources on poverty. Components of family income are sequentially added and measured against families' poverty thresholds, as one moves from the top line of the chart to subsequent lines below.[49] Starting with the top line, the effect on poverty of family earnings alone is depicted. Poverty measures based on earned income alone give an indication of the labor market's effect on poverty, in context of other sources of income individuals, families, and households might receive. Moving to the second line down, the effect of earnings plus all other cash income other than cash welfare (AFDC, TANF, or state General Assistance) is shown. Adding cash welfare, the third line down, to those income sources shown above, completes the accounting of pre-tax cash income that is used under the "official" U.S. poverty definition.

Addition of Income from Sources Not Included in the "Official" U.S. Poverty Measure

As noted above, the "official" U.S. poverty definition is based on families' pre-tax cash income. It excludes a number of benefits families receive, such as Food Stamp/SNAP benefits, and refundable tax credits, such as the EITC and ACTC, nor does it take into account taxes families might pay, in the form of federal payroll (FICA) taxes and federal and state income taxes. A congressionally commissioned study, issued in 1995 by a National Academy of Sciences (NAS) expert panel proposed major changes to the way in which poverty is measured in the U.S.[50] After 15 years of study, the Department of Commerce Economic and Statistics Administration, under an Office of Management and Budget (OMB) sponsored initiative, announced that the Census Bureau, in coordination with the Bureau of Labor Statistics (BLS), will develop a Supplemental Poverty Measure (SPM), using NAS panel recommendations and subsequent research as a framework.[51] The proposed measure will supplement, rather than replace, the current poverty measure, which will continue to be deemed the "official" statistical measure of poverty in the United States. Among features of the proposed SPM is that it would include a number of in-kind and tax benefits in the measure. The Census Bureau has yet to release a regular poverty series based on the SPM, due to lack of funding. Absent the availability of an alternate, supplemental, measure to the official one, the following poverty estimates include income sources in addition to those used under the official measure, and compares those combined sources to the official poverty income thresholds.

In addition to the income sources used by the "official" poverty measure, a number of other income sources are sequentially added to estimate their anti-poverty effects under more comprehensive income definitions. For example, the market value of Food Stamp/SNAP benefits is added to pre-tax cash income, to assess their antipoverty effects. Next, the EITC is added in, net of any FICA, federal, and state income taxes (including state refundable tax credits). The poverty reducing effect of the ACTC is then assessed, followed by economic stimulus and recovery payments families may have received in 2008 and 2009, respectively.

A cautionary note is in order with regards to assessing the effects tax credits such as the EITC and ACTC on family income and poverty. The effect of the credits shown in the CPS/ASEC are estimates of the amount of the EITC and/or ACTC benefits families would have been eligible to receive based on their calendar year (i.e., tax year) income. However, while the tax credits' effects are shown for the depicted year in which the credits are earned, families would not actually receive the credits until early in the following year, after filing their federal income tax forms.

Finally, the bottom-most line shows the effects of counting all income in the household in which the single mother lives, not just that of her related family members, and compares it to "household low-income thresholds." The household low-income thresholds used here are scaled the same way as Census Bureau family income poverty thresholds, but are based on household (rather than family) size and composition. It is important to note that official poverty measurement is based on a family concept, which assumes that family members share income and economies of scale that result from shared living arrangements. It is generally agreed among researchers that assumptions regarding income sharing and shared economies of scale among related family members, who have ties based on blood, marriage, and adoption, do not apply to the same extent among unrelated household members. Consequently, these estimates of household low-income status likely overstate the effect of household income on reducing poverty among families headed by single mothers.

Effect of Earnings and Other Non-Welfare Cash Income on Poverty

Figure 13 shows that between 1993 and 2000, single mothers' poverty, based on family earnings alone (*top line*), fell from 56.2% to 40.8%, reaching an historic low for the 23-year period. Their "earned-income poverty rate" rose consequent to two recessions, reaching 44.3% in 2004, and rising again from 44.7% in 2007 to 48.3% in 2009. Adding other cash income, except cash welfare (*second line down*), to family earnings, reduces poverty in 1993 from 56.2% (*top line*) to 47.4% (*line 2*), and in 2009 from 48.3% to 38.0%.

Effect of Cash Welfare on Poverty

Cash welfare benefits have only a small impact on the poverty rate, as these benefits generally are not sufficient, even when combined with other cash income, to lift families above the federal poverty threshold. In the vast majority of states the level of earnings or other cash income at which states' cash welfare benefits under AFDC/TANF become unavailable for a family are well below the poverty line. For example, in July 2009, in only five states and the District of Columbia could a single mother with two children have earnings at or above the poverty line and still continue to receive TANF cash assistance after one year of benefit receipt.[52] Consequently, cash welfare benefits have little impact on the poverty rate. The addition of cash welfare (*line 3*, representing the official income definition for measuring poverty) reduces poverty only slightly: from 47.4% (*line 2*) to 45.2% (*line 3*) in 1993, and from 38.0% to 37.6% in 2009. Nonetheless, cash welfare benefits can have a significant impact on the level of poor families' incomes, affecting the degree to which their incomes fall below the poverty income standard. This impact is not captured by changes in the poverty rate as shown in Figure 13.

The Invisible Safety Net—Effect on Poverty of Counting Selected Income Sources Not Included in the "Official" Poverty Measure

As noted above, the "official" U.S. poverty measure counts only families' pre-tax cash income for purposes of poverty determination. Inclusion of selected benefits, such as food assistance, in the form of Food Stamp/SNAP benefits, the refundable EITC, and the partially refundable ACTC, allows for a more comprehensive assessment of the role of government policy in addressing vulnerable families income needs.

Effect of Food Stamp/SNAP Benefits on Poverty

SNAP benefits played a substantively larger role in reducing poverty among single mothers and their families in 2009, in the wake of the past recession, than in any year earlier. The fourth line from the top in Figure 13 shows the effect on the poverty rate of single mothers by counting the value of Food Stamp/SNAP benefits. The line shows that Food Stamps/SNAP reduced the poverty rate of single mothers from about 2 to 3 percentage points over most of the period (compare the reduction in poverty from *line 3* to *line 4*). In 2009, however, SNAP benefits nearly offset the rise in pre-tax cash income poverty (i.e., the "official" poverty measure) from 2008. Whereas on a pre-tax cash-only basis, poverty among single mothers and their families increased from 33.8% in 2008 to 37.6% in 2009 (*line 3*), SNAP benefits, when added to cash income, caused the poverty rate of single mothers to remain essentially level over the two years (33.% in 2008, and 33.5% in 2009).

The increased role of SNAP benefits in addressing the rising cash income deficiency of single mothers in the wake of the recent recession, reflects not only an increase in the take-up rate of SNAP benefits by low-income families headed by single mothers, seen earlier in Figure 12, but also the legislatively enacted increase of SNAP benefit payments to needy households under ARRA. As noted earlier (section entitled: "Supplemental Nutrition Assistance Program (SNAP/Food Stamp) Benefits"), ARRA SNAP provisions resulted in an average 15% increase in monthly SNAP benefits going into effect in April 2009.

Net Effect of the EITC on Poverty

The EITC has had a comparatively large poverty reducing effect on single mothers and their families since 1993 legislative expansions to the credit took effect. The poverty reducing effect of the EITC[53] is shown net of FICA, federal, and state income taxes (including refundable state tax credits) (*line5*), when added to family cash income and Food Stamp/SNAP benefits (*line 4*). As discussed earlier (section entitled: "EITC Expansions—"Making Work Pay""), a major expansion of the EITC, passed by Congress in 1993 and phased in between 1994 and 1996, increased the amount of the EITC work bonus families might receive. The anti-poverty effectiveness of the EITC was six times greater in 2009 than in 1993.[54] In combination with Food Stamp/SNAP benefits, the EITC has kept the poverty rate of single mothers and their families level since 2004, whereas under the official measure, poverty is shown to have increased.

As receipt of the EITC is conditioned on earnings, the growing impact of the EITC in part reflects the rise in work rates among single mothers. Among those who are working and poor (before counting the EITC), the EITC helps lift the income of some above the poverty line. Although the EITC expansion provided additional income to low-income families who were already working, it may also have helped induce increased employment among family heads with low to moderate earnings potential, and thus contributed to the lower levels of poverty based on earned income alone, that have been evidenced since 1993 (shown as the top line in the chart).

Note too, that to the extent that changes in cash welfare programs in recent years have encouraged work (such as work requirements and increased earnings disregards), these changes may have had a direct effect on poverty by increasing the incidence of work (earnings), which in turn resulted in expanded EITC receipt among single mothers.

Effect of the ACTC on Poverty

The Additional Child Tax Credit (ACTC) (the refundable portion of the Child Tax Credit) can provide a refund to tax filers with one or more qualified children, even if they have no federal income tax liability. Overall, tax filers may receive a Child Tax Credit (CTC) up to $1,000 per qualifying child. If the CTC is greater than the amount of income tax owed, the tax filer may be eligible to claim the ACTC. As noted earlier (section entitled: "Tax Rebates and Credits"), The Economic Stabilization Act of 2008 (ESSA, P.L. 110-343) reduced the ACTC's refundable income limit from $12,050 to $8,500 for 2008. ARRA (P.L. 111-5) further reduced the credit's refundable income limit from a scheduled $12,550 in 2009, to $3,000 for 2009 and 2010.

As shown above (Figure 13), the lowered ACTC refundable income limit for 2009 resulted in a marked reduction in poverty among single mothers and their families, reducing their poverty rate from 29.6%, before counting the credit (5th *line down*), to 27.9% after counting the credit (*6th line down*). Prior to the legislative changes discussed above, most poor families were beyond the credit's reach. Moreover, ARRA provisions, when combined with EITC, SNAP benefits, and cash income, resulted in a net decline in poverty from 2008 to 2009, which sharply contrasts the observed increase in poverty based on cash income alone (*line 3*).

Effect of Federal Economic Stimulus and Economic Recovery Payments on Poverty

In addition to the changes to the EITC and ACTC made as part of legislative action to stimulate the economy, the Census Bureau provides estimates of economic stimulus payments families may have received in 2008, and economic recovery payments in 2009 (see earlier discussion, "Tax Rebates and Credits"). The effects of economic stimulus and economic recovery payments in 2008 and 2009 on single mothers' poverty status are shown above (Figure 13). When added to *line 6*, above, economic stimulus payments in 2008 reduced single mothers' poverty rate from 29.4% to 28.3% in 2008, and from 27.9% to 27.3% in 2009.

When all taken together, the ACTC and economic stimulus and recovery payments resulted in net reductions in poverty among single mothers and their families from 2007 to 2008, and from 2008 to 2009. Consequently, whereas poverty under the "official" pre-tax cash definition increased for single mothers from 2008 to 2009, under a more comprehensive definition which includes Food Stamp/SNAP benefits, the effects of the EITC (net of taxes), the ACTC, and economic stimulus and recovery payments, their incidence of poverty actually declined. Moreover, whereas the "official" poverty rate for single mothers and their families of 37.6% in 2009 was 5.8 percentage points above its all-time low of 31.8%, in 2000, their poverty rate based on a more comprehensive income definition that takes Food Stamp/SNAP benefits, taxes and refundable tax credits, and economic recovery payments into account, was 27.3% in 2009, just ½ of a percentage point above its all-time low of 26.8% in 2000.

Effect of Unrelated Household Member's Income on Poverty

The household low-income line (*bottom line*, Figure 13) shows that if all household members' income is counted, as though shared equally among household members, the poverty rate among single mothers would drop by at most 3 to 4 percentage points over the 1987 to 2009 period. Using the household, as opposed to the family, as the economic unit for determining poverty reduces the post in-kind transfer, post-tax, poverty rate in 1993 from 40.7% to 36.8% and, in 2009, from 27.3% to 23.1%. Again, this is most likely an overstatement of the possible effect that shared household living arrangements might have on single mothers' poverty status because of the uncertainty about the extent to which such income is actually shared.

Comparison of the Effects of Earnings, Transfers, and Taxes on Poverty, by Single Mothers' Work Status

The analysis above examines the effects of earning, transfers, taxes, and other income on families headed by single mothers. Here, the effects are broken out by whether or not mothers worked at any time during the year. There is a stark contrast in the incidence of poverty among single mothers who worked at any time during a year, and those who did not. Moreover, selected income "safety-net" programs have quite different effects in reducing poverty among the two groups, as shown in Figure 14 and Figure 15, respectively. The figures show, for example, *that mothers who worked* at any time during the year were less likely to be poor based on their *earnings alone* than *mothers who did not work* based on *total household income.*

In comparing across the two figures, it should be noted that the scale shown in Figure 14 ranges from 0% to 50%, while that of Figure 15 ranges from 50% to 100%, as if it were stacked above Figure 14 (i.e., the two figures scales are the same with regard to relative range of their vertical axes, but the levels at which those axes start differ).

Several observations follow.

Single Mothers Who Worked During the Year - Figure 14

Effects of Selected Cash Income Sources on Poverty

- Among single mothers who worked during the year, their incidence of poverty based on earned income alone was at a low in 2000, and has increased markedly since 2005 (*top line*).
- Cash income from sources other than UI and cash welfare (*second line down*) has had a relatively consistent effect of reducing their

poverty rate from that measured by earnings alone, ranging from 6 to 8 percentage points over the 23-year period.

- UI benefits in 2009 reduced their poverty rate by about 1 percentage point, which was about the same as in 2002, the previous peak year of UI poverty reduction.
- Adding in SSI benefits has little effect on poverty reduction among this group, largely by virtue that mothers worked during the year, and were consequently unlikely to have had an SSI qualifying disability (although, other members of their family might).
- AFDC, TANF and GA have very little impact on poverty reduction among single mothers who worked in recent years, but had more measurable effects in the first part of the 23-year period, when poor mothers were more likely to combine work with welfare (refer back to Figure 11).
- Based on the "official" poverty measure which takes into account most sources of pre-tax cash income families receive, the poverty rate among single mothers in 2009 was 2.8 percentage points higher than in 2001—an historic low for the period.

Effects on Poverty of Selected Income Sources Not Included in the "Official" Poverty Measure

- Food Stamp and SNAP benefit receipt have had a sizeable effect on poverty reduction, and in 2009 reversed the trend in poverty based on cash income alone.
- The EITC (net of FICA and federal and state income taxes) has contributed to substantial reductions in poverty among working single mothers, especially after 1993 legislated expansions to the credit began taking effect. In 2009, net EITC among working single mothers reduced their post SNAP benefit poverty rate by 5.5 percentage points, from 22.5% to 17.0%.
- ARRA's reduction of the ACTC's refundable income limit to $3,000, effective in 2009, is readily apparent by the substantially larger decrease in poverty resulting from the credit, than in earlier years. In 2009, the ACTC accounted for an additional 2.1 percentage point reduction in poverty beyond that of the post-EITC poverty level.
- After including the ACTC, the incidence of poverty among single mothers with any work during the year reached an historic low in 2009, in spite of the effect of the recession on official poverty, which in that same year was at an eight-year high.

- In 2009, after taking into account SNAP benefits, net EITC, the ACTC, and Economic Stimulus and Recovery Payments, the poverty rate of single mothers who worked sometime during the year was 14.2%, a full 12 percentage points below the "official" measure (26.2%) and 3.1 percentage points below its 2002 level of 17.3%.
- If the income of all unrelated household members is included as income, the poverty rate among working single mothers is estimated at 11.2% in 2009, which compares to an "official" poverty rate of 26.2%.

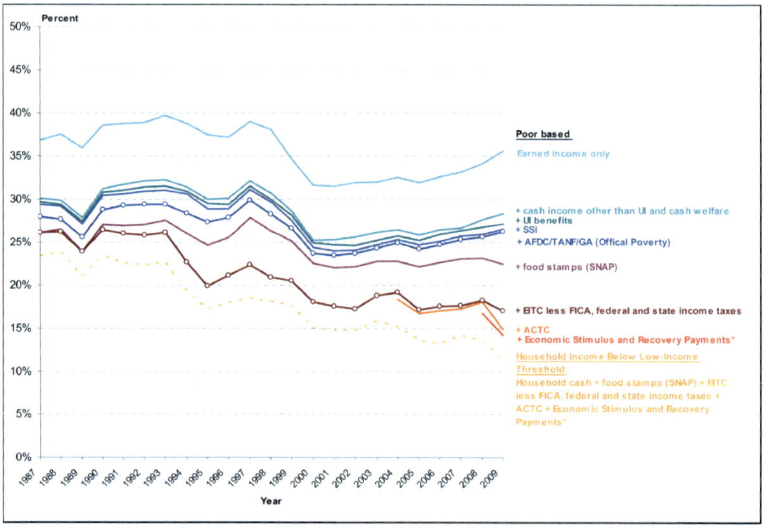

Source: Prepared by the Congressional Research Service (CRS) based on analysis of U.S. Census Bureau 1988 to 2010 Current Population Survey (CPS) Annual Social and Economic Supplement (ASEC) data. See Table C-12 for supporting data.

* Census Bureau estimates of Economic Stimulus Payments received in 2008 and Economic Recovery Payments received in 2009.

Figure 14. Single Mothers Who Worked at Any Time During the Year: Effects of Earnings, Transfers, and Taxes on Family Poverty and Household Low-Income Status, 1987 to 2009.

- *Note that working mothers could also incur work-related expenses (e.g., child care, transportation, uniforms) that are not accounted for here. Inclusion of such expenses, if available, would result in somewhat higher poverty rates than those shown here.*

Single Mothers Who Did Not Work during the Year - Figure 15

As a precautionary reminder, the reader should note that the origin of the vertical axis begins at a poverty rate of 50%.

Effects of Selected Cash Income Sources on Poverty

- The top-most line indicates that even though single mothers themselves did not work during the year, and thus had no earnings, other related family members may have worked, accounting for an "earnings-only" poverty level around 90% in the pre welfare reform era (1996 and earlier), and around 85% since 2000.
- The next line down, which includes most all other sources of income other than UI benefits and cash welfare, shows a somewhat greater reduction in poverty in the TANF era (about 10 percentage points), than in the pre welfare reform era (about 5 percentage points). In part, this may be due to a somewhat greater tendency of nonworking single mothers to be living in "extended" families (i.e., living with family members other than just their children) in the post welfare reform era, than before. For example, in 1996, 24% of nonworking single mothers lived in extended family settings, but by 2000, 33% were living in such settings.[55]
- The figure shows UI benefits, when added to earnings and other cash income from the line above, accounted for a 2 percentage point reduction in poverty in 2009, over twice the effect in 2002, the previous peak year of UI poverty reduction for this group.
- Comparing the relative effects of SSI and TANF/AFDC/GA on poverty over the period, SSI has assumed a greater role in poverty reduction among nonworking single mothers in the TANF, than in the pre-TANF, era, and the role of TANF in reducing poverty among this group is substantially less than what it was under AFDC.
- Examining just the trend in "official" poverty among nonworking single mothers, their poverty rate in the post welfare reform era has averaged 8 percentage points below what it was under AFDC. In 2002, which marked an historic low poverty rate for this group, their poverty rate (66.9%) was nearly 14 percentage points below their peak rate of 80.8% in 1991. In 2009, 69.9% of nonworking single mothers were poor—still well below their pre welfare reform levels.

Effects on Poverty of Selected Income Sources Not Included in the "Official" Poverty Measure

- Food Stamp/SNAP benefits appear to have had a somewhat smaller effect on poverty reduction among nonworking single mothers in the post-welfare reform era (2.7 percentage point reduction, on average) than earlier (about 3.6 percentage point reduction, on average, in the pre welfare reform era). However, in 2009, reflecting ARRA's SNAP benefit provisions, discussed earlier ("Supplemental Nutrition Assistance Program (SNAP/Food Stamp) Benefits"), SNAP benefits reduced poverty for this group from the "official" poverty rate of 69.9%, to 64.7%, a 5.2 percentage point reduction.

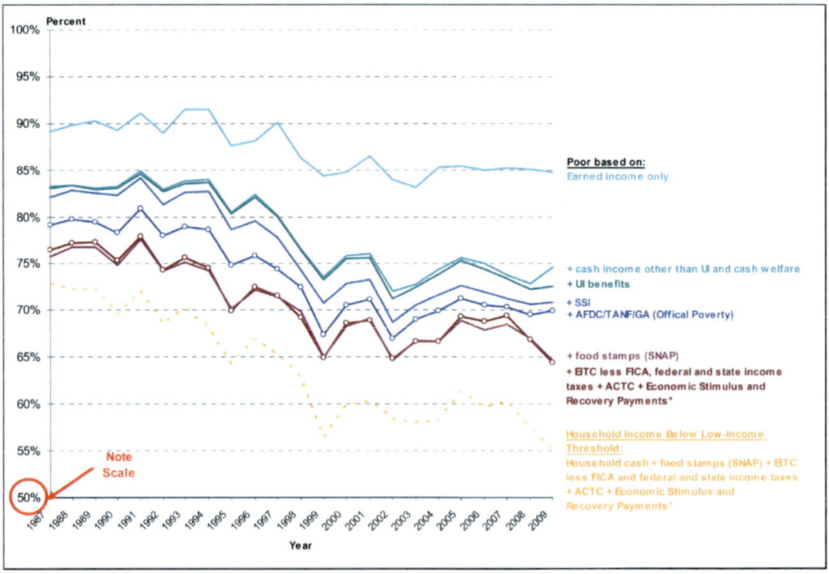

Source: Prepared by the Congressional Research Service (CRS) based on analysis of U.S. Census Bureau 1988 to 2010 Current Population Survey (CPS) Annual Social and Economic Supplement (ASEC) data. See Table C-13 for supporting data.

* Census Bureau estimates of Economic Stimulus Payments received in 2008 and Economic Recovery Payments received in 2009.

Figure 15. Single Mothers Who Did Not Work During the Year: Effects of Earnings, Transfers, and Taxes on Family Poverty and Household Low-Income Status, 1987 to 2009.

- In that these mothers did not work during the year, the figure shows refundable and partially refundable tax provisions have had very little measurable effect on poverty reduction for this group; nor have economic stimulus or recovery payments. In fact, the after-tax poverty line is at times above the Food Stamp/SNAP line, indicating that some poor families had members with a tax liability, net of any credits.
- If the income of all unrelated household members is included as income, the poverty rate among nonworking single mothers is estimated at 55.1% in 2009. Counting unrelated household members' income reduced poverty among nonworking single mothers by 9.6 percentage points in 2009, compared to 3.6 percentage points in 1987. This largely reflects what has been a growing tendency of nonworking single mothers to be living with other unrelated household members. In 2009, for example, 20% of nonworking single mothers were living with other unrelated family members, of which over four-fifths were designated as "cohabiting partners" (see Table C-14). In comparison, about 9% of nonworking single mothers lived with unrelated family members in 1987.[56]

DISCUSSION/CONCLUSION

CRS analysis of 23 years of U.S. Census Bureau data presented in this report shows a dramatic transformation in single mothers' welfare, work, and poverty status over the period. The period has seen a marked *structural change* in the provision of benefits under a number of programs that contribute to the fabric of the nation's "income safety net." In turn, single mothers' *behavior has changed* markedly over the period, with more mothers working, and fewer relying on cash welfare to support themselves and their children, in part in response to structural changes to income "safety-net" programs. Poverty under the official U.S. poverty measure, which is based on pre-tax cash income, shows that since 2000, which marked an historic low, the poverty rate among single mothers increased in step with two recessions. By 2009, the official poverty rate for single mothers had reached a post-2000 high, but in spite of two recessions, was still below pre-1996 welfare reform levels. Using a more comprehensive income definition than that used by the official poverty measure indicates that poverty among single mothers and their children in 2009, rather than having increased since 2000, was at or near a 23-year low when Food Stamp/SNAP benefits and work-related refundable tax credits are taken into account. In particular, congressional action in response to the recession, which increased SNAP benefits and extended the reach of refundable tax credits, contributed to a decline in poverty among single mothers and their children in the midst of the recession.

Transformation of Income Safety-Net Programs toward Work-Conditioned Support

Since the eve of 1996 welfare reform, work-conditioned requirements for individuals' receipt of government assistance have become more prevalent. Prior to 1996-welfare reform, federal law (The Family Support Act of 1988; P.L. 100-485) had extended work requirements (which included work preparation activities, such as education and training) to mothers receiving AFDC to mothers with a child as young as three, and at state option, to mothers with a child as young as age one. Child care funding was increased to make it possible for mothers to go to work. A number of states experimented with changes to their welfare programs under waivers of federal rules, granted by DHHS. Among the features tested under waiver authority were efforts to strengthen work requirements, experiments to test models of facilitating the transition from welfare to work, and the use of sanctions for noncompliance with welfare rules, among others. Expansions to the EITC, under both President G.H.W. Bush, and Clinton, increased the financial rewards of work, through earnings supplements administered through the tax system. The EITC helped to offset the welfare income loss, or implicit tax, that mothers might face as they moved from welfare to work.

The 1996 welfare reform law repealed the 61-year-old AFDC program, replacing it with TANF. TANF ended the entitlement of low-income families with children to federal assistance. It limits the provision of federal assistance under the program to five years[57]—states are allowed to set shorter time limits. Under TANF, states no longer receive an open-ended federal matching grant, as they did under AFDC, but rather a fixed dollar block grant (with the possible addition of recession-related contingency funds). Adults must be engaged in approved "work activities" within two years of initial TANF receipt, subject to sanction for noncompliance. Under TANF, federal work participation standards (i.e., "work-requirements") apply to states' TANF caseloads, and adult recipients are required to be engaged in work, or work-related activities after two years of benefit receipt. TANF has provided states increased flexibility and limited federal requirements, compared to AFDC, but with fixed federal dollars.

Since 1996 welfare reform, cash welfare support for "earnings poor" mothers and their children has contracted, whereas work-based support has increased. The EITC, for example, has a direct effect on poverty reduction, by encouraging work, increasing earnings, and reducing reliance on cash welfare. One estimate suggests that single mothers employment in 1996 was 7 percentage points higher than it would have been otherwise, absent the EITC.[58] This "work/earnings inducing" effect of EITC among single mothers is captured in official poverty statistics, as part of families' earnings, but the credit itself—the earnings supplement which induces work and earnings—is not. Likewise, the ACTC may also have a potential work inducing effect among single mothers, but, like the EITC, the effects of the credit itself on poverty reduction are not measured under the official poverty income definition. Additionally, through earnings, working individuals not only gain potential access to tax benefits, such as the EITC and ACTC, which with full-time work exceeds cash welfare assistance they might have received by not working, but also earn credit towards insurance coverage under Unemployment Insurance, as well as Social Security retirement, disability, and death benefits for themselves, their dependents, and survivors.

The report shows that receipt of cash welfare (AFDC, TANF, or General Assistance) has declined substantially among single mothers since the passage of TANF, and their engagement in work has increased (Figure 8). The transformation from welfare dependency to work appears to have begun in the years immediately preceding 1996 welfare reform, as the economy prospered, and as a number of work supports (e.g., EITC, and child care assistance) were strengthened. Moreover, under the official U.S. poverty measure, the poverty rate of single mothers (Figure 6), and that of their children (Figure 4), has consistently been lower since welfare reform, than before. Prior to TANF, *poor* single mothers were more likely to be receiving cash welfare (AFDC or GA) than to be working; after passage of TANF, just the opposite was true: *poor* single mothers were more likely to be working than receiving cash welfare (TANF or GA) (Figure 11).

TANF and other work-promoting policies have helped to reduce poverty among single mothers and their children through increased earnings. Based on earnings alone, poverty among single mothers who worked reached an historic low for the period, in 2000 (Figure 14), as did their poverty rate based on total pre-tax cash income, under the "official" U.S. poverty measure. Following the

2000 recession, poverty among working single mothers increased slightly, and much more so since 2007, in step with the 2007-2009 recession.

Cash Welfare's Residual Safety-Net Role

Welfare reform ended the provision of cash assistance as an entitlement, by replacing AFDC with a fixed dollar block grant for the provision of Temporary Assistance for Needy Families. Under TANF, a greater share of funds goes toward services (child care, social services) either directly, or through transfers to other programs (CCDBG, Title XX Social Services) than towards direct cash support. While many of these services may help to reduce dependency, and promote self-sufficiency through work, receipt of cash assistance has shrunk markedly in the TANF era. While TANF caseloads increased modestly in 2009 and 2010 in response to the recession, they are at a fraction of what they were at their peak, just prior to 1996 welfare reform, and reflect levels not seen in over 40 years.

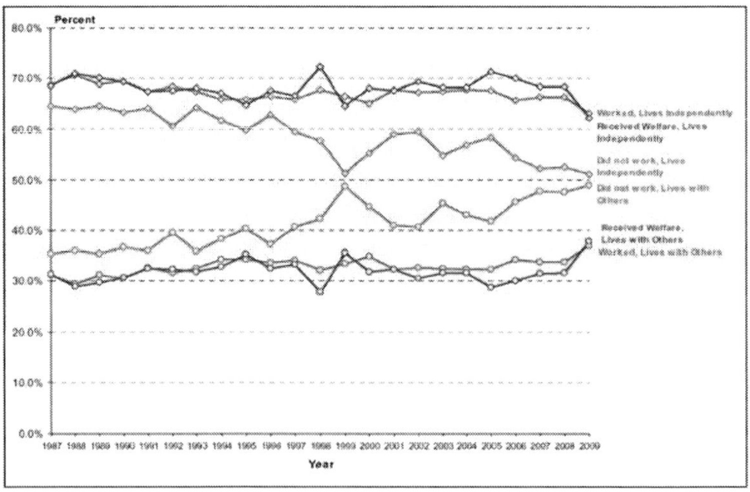

Source: Prepared by the Congressional Research Service (CRS) based on analysis of U.S. Census Bureau 1988 to 2010 Current Population Survey (CPS) Annual Social and Economic Supplement (ASEC) data. See Table C-14 for supporting data.

Figure 16. Single Mothers' Living Arrangements, by Mothers' Work and Welfare Status 1987 to 2009.

The marked decline in cash welfare caseloads since the eve of 1996 welfare reform, reflects an apparent behavioral shift among many single mothers with respect to work and welfare, with more selecting the former than the later. A restructuring of income safety-net programs to support work is likely to have contributed to single mothers' changed behavior. The EITC appears to be an import component of the restructured safety net, as it encourages work, even among mothers whose earnings prospects at initial job entry are low. In most states, full time work at the minimum wage provides income sufficient for a mother to work her way off of cash welfare. In lieu of cash welfare, a single mother working full time at the minimum wage will receive the EITC. Additionally, in 2009 through 2012, due to legislative changes relating to the recession and recovery, she will be eligible for the ACTC, which provides additional income support for her children.

Living Arrangements as an Alternative to Welfare

Cash welfare receipt and poverty among single mothers is lower since TANF's enactment than before. Some of this effect appears to be due to an increase in work among single mothers. However, even among *nonworking* mothers, their receipt of cash assistance and incidence of poverty under the official measure is lower since welfare reform. It appears that other family members' earnings and other cash income has contributed to the lower poverty rates of *nonworking* single mothers in the post-AFDC era (see the earlier discussion, "Single Mothers Who Did Not Work During the Year - Figure 15") .

In spite of policies to increase work among single mothers, not all single mothers work, and lack of work contributes significantly to the likelihood that they and their children will be poor. However, *poor* nonworking single mothers are much less likely to be receiving cash welfare assistance under TANF than they did under AFDC (Figure 11). In the post-AFDC era, nonworking single mothers are somewhat more likely to live in extended family settings than before.[59] It appears that living with other relatives helps to reduce their reliance on welfare and incidence of poverty under the official poverty measure. Moreover, nonworking single mothers are considerably more likely (more than twice as likely) to live with other unrelated family members in the post-AFDC era than before, although income of these unrelated household members is not taken into account in determining poverty status.[60]

These alternative living arrangements might help provide an alternative to cash welfare receipt for some single mothers. Figure 16 suggests that this statement has some bearing. The figure depicts single mothers by their work and welfare status, according to whether they live independently with just their children, or whether they live with others, either in an extended family household with other family members than just her children, or with one or more other, unrelated, persons, including a cohabiting partner. The figure shows that among mothers who worked, or received welfare during the year, the majority (roughly 65% to 70%) lived independently over the period; a minority (roughly 30% to 35%) lived with others (extended family and/or one or more unrelated persons). Interestingly, both mothers who worked, as well as those who received welfare, were equally as likely to live independently, as not, over the period.

In contrast, nonworking single mothers, as a group, are less likely than their working counterparts to live independently than mothers who work or receive welfare during the year. In the pre-1996 welfare reform era, nonworking single mothers were slightly less likely to live independently (roughly 65% to 60%), than their working counterparts (roughly 70% to 65%) or those who received welfare (also, roughly 70% to 65%). Note that some of these nonworking mothers may also have received cash welfare during the year, as evidenced earlier in Figure 8. Welfare receipt among nonworking single mothers may have contributed to their ability to live independently, apart from other relatives or nonrelatives. While many single mothers selected work as an alternative to welfare in the years immediately following 1996 welfare reform, others appear to have found alternative living arrangements instead. In 1996, 62% of nonworking single mothers were living independently, three years later, only 52% were. Most of this change in living arrangements was due to an increase in nonworking single mothers' increased tendency to live in extended family households, with other relatives (see Table C-14), with the share increasing from 24% in 1996, to 33% by 1999, and then ebbing to 27% by 2001. In more recent years, at least since 2005, nonworking single mothers have shown a greater tendency to be living with other nonrelatives, of which most are cohabiting partners (see Table C-14). Whereas in 1987, 65% of nonworking single mothers were living in independent households, by 2009, only about half (52%) were. In part, cash welfare in the pre-welfare reform era may have helped some single mothers to live in independent family settings. Stricter requirements and time limits in the post-reform era may have contributed to some mothers' consideration of living arrangements as an alternative to cash welfare receipt.

Illness or Disability among Nonworking Single Mothers

Nonworking single mothers are much more likely to attribute illness or disability as the reason for not working in the post-welfare reform era, than before. This is consistent with the somewhat greater role of SSI relative to other cash welfare (AFDC/TANF/GA) since welfare reform. One conjecture is that single mothers who are most able to work, are doing so in the post-welfare reform era, and that with support from the EITC, even those with comparatively low earnings capacity (e.g., earnings poor), have sought work over welfare. Those remaining, who are not engaged in work, may be less able to work, as indicated by a higher self-reported incidence of illness or disability. In the pre-welfare reform era, roughly 10% of nonworking single mothers reported "illness or disability" as the primary reason for not working during the year (Figure 17), and roughly 70% reported "taking care of home or family" as the primary reason.[61] In the post-welfare reform era, the share of nonworking single mothers who self-reported "illness or disability" as the reason for not working is about three times higher than before welfare reform; the share who reported "taking care of home or family" as the primary reason for not working has fallen from roughly 70% to about 50% since welfare reform.

Cash Welfare Receipt among Ill or Disabled Nonworking Single Mothers

Whereas nonworking single mothers have a greater tendency to report illness or disability as the primary reason for having not worked during the year, cash safety-net programs in the form of AFDC/TANF and SSI appear to be assisting a smaller share of such mothers in the post-welfare reform era, than before. Moreover, the number of single mothers reporting illness or disability in 2009 has more than doubled since 1987 (see Figure 18). In the pre-welfare reform era, roughly 70% to 80% of nonworking single mothers who reported illness or disability as the reason for not working were being assisted by AFDC, SSI, or both—in 2009, 50% were. The SSI program taken alone (not counting in combination with AFDC/TANF receipt) accounts for a considerably larger share of nonworking ill or disabled single mothers in the post-welfare reform era (roughly double) than before. In turn, the share reporting receipt of AFDC/TANF, either alone, or in combination with SSI, has fallen by more than half since welfare reform, with about 60% reporting AFDC in the pre-welfare reform era, and about 30% reporting TANF, after.

While a larger share of single mothers who are able to work appear to be engaged in work or looking for work in the post-welfare reform era than before, among the smaller residual who are not, a greater share report illness or disability as the primary reason for being out of the labor market. In 2009, of the 679,000 single mothers who reported no work during the year, roughly half (346,000) reported neither receiving SSI nor TANF/GA assistance. The nature of these mothers' reported illness or disability is not known, nor is it known whether they have sought and been denied government assistance. Whether and how these mothers might be falling through cracks in the income safety-net is a question of policy interest, and possible concern.

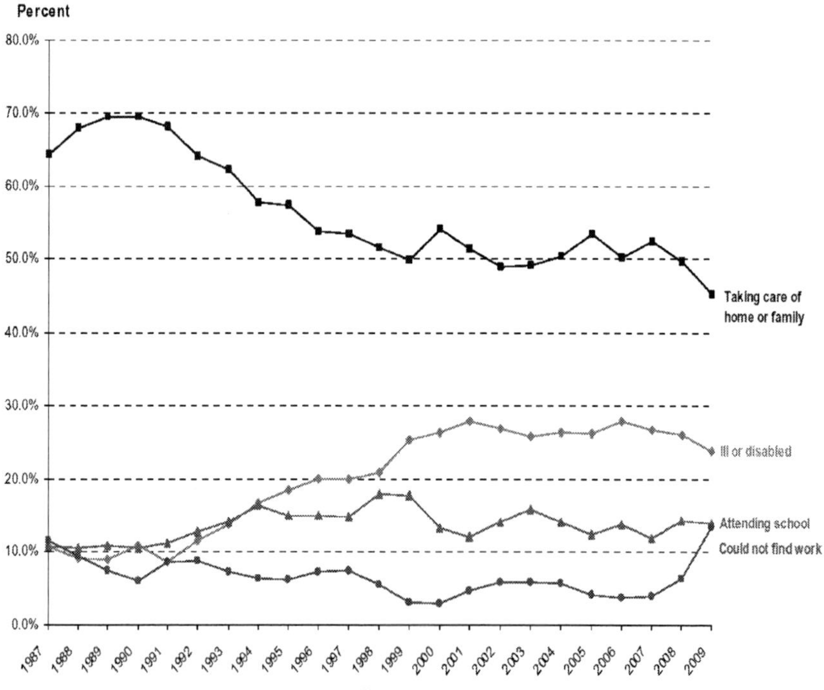

Source: Prepared by the Congressional Research Service (CRS) based on analysis of U.S. Census Bureau 1988 to 2010 Current Population Survey (CPS) Annual Social and Economic Supplement (ASEC) data. See Table C-16 for supporting data.

Figure 17. Single Mothers Who Did Not Work During the Year, by Self-Reported Reason for Not Working 1987 to 2009.

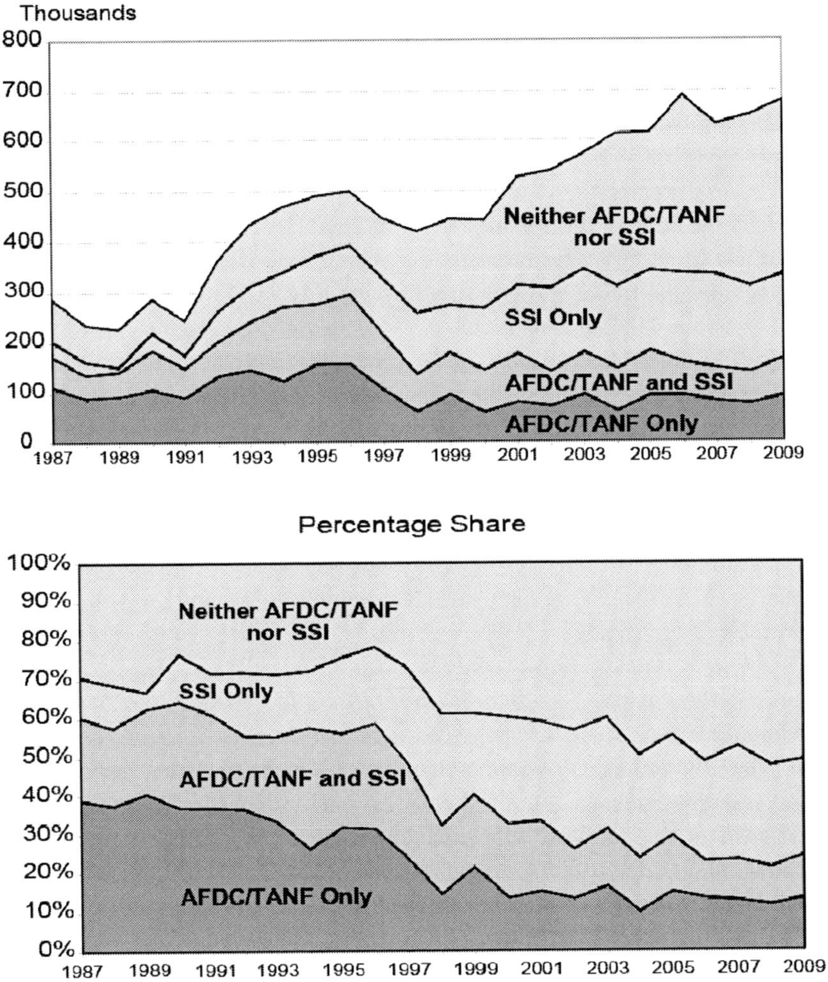

Source: Prepared by the Congressional Research Service (CRS) based on analysis of U.S. Census Bureau 1988 to 2010 Current Population Survey (CPS) Annual Social and Economic Supplement (ASEC) data. See Table C-16 for supporting data.

Figure 18. Nonworking Single Mothers with Self-Reported "Illness or Disability" as the Primary Reason for Not Working, by Cash Welfare Recipiency Status 1987 to 2009.

The Work-Based Income Safety Net in Times of Recession and Recovery

The official U.S. poverty measure provides little insight as to how the transformed work-based income safety net has performed since the expansions to EITC in the early 1990s, and 1996 welfare reform, in reducing poverty. As shown in the body of this report, a very different story from the one offered by the official poverty measure emerges by using an expanded income measure that includes the EITC, and more recently, the ACTC, refundable tax credits, and Food Stamp/SNAP assistance.

By the official measure, poverty would appear to have increased substantially among single mothers and their children from 2000, in step with two recessions. Official poverty among single mothers and their children, while having reached a recent peak in 2009, is still below that of the pre-1996 welfare reform. Given that single mothers unemployment rates in 2010 (shown earlier, in Figure 9) are above 2009 levels (average annual unemployment rate of 12.3% in 2010, compared to 11.5% in 2009) one would expect the official poverty rate for single mothers and their children to continue to rise in 2010 (see Table C-8).

The Invisible Safety-Net - Benefits not Officially Counted toward Poverty Reduction

While the provision of cash welfare has fallen dramatically under TANF, poor and lower-income families with earnings are more likely to receive assistance in the form of supplemental nutrition assistance, or refundable income credits administered through federal and state tax systems. Neither in-kind benefits, such as those provided through Food Stamps/SNAP, nor refundable credits, such as the EITC, or partially refundable ACTC, are counted as income under the official U.S. poverty measure, yet these three programs are among the ten largest, in terms of federal spending for people with low income.[62] Clearly, these programs constitute important strands in the nation's income safety-net, yet they generally are not taken into account when assessing its strengths and weaknesses. Under an alternative, more comprehensive measure of poverty than the official one, which includes the net effects of refundable tax credits and Food Stamp/SNAP benefits, a quite different assessment of the effects of the safety net on poverty among single mothers and their children emerges.

While the Census Bureau publishes a number of alternative, experimental poverty measures, in addition to the official one, those measures are typically not released until several months after the release of the official measure. The alternative poverty measures typically do not receive the same focus by researchers and the public as does the official measure, in part due to the delay in their release, but also due to the numerous alternative measures that are released, each reflecting varying, often technical, assumptions. A proposed Supplemental Poverty Measure being jointly developed by the Census Bureau and Bureau of Labor Statistics, under the direction of OMB, is intended to stand out among the alternative measures as the "preferred" alternative measure, to supplement the official measure. Among other things, the proposed Supplemental Poverty Measure would provide a more comprehensive gauge of the effects of income safety-net programs on poverty than the official measure.

Progress towards achieving the often elusive and conflicting dual goals of reducing child poverty and cash welfare dependency is only partially apparent under the official U.S. poverty measure, but much more so under an alternative, more comprehensive income measure. Under the official poverty measure, poverty among single mothers in 2009 (37.6%) was 5.8 percentage points above its historic low for the period (31.8% in 2000). In contrast, under a more comprehensive income measure which takes into account SNAP benefits, refundable tax credits (the EITC and ACTC) net of taxes, and economic stimulus and recovery payments, poverty among single mothers in 2009 (27.3%) fell to a near all-time low (26.6% in 2002), in spite of the severe 2007-2009 recession (Figure 13). Similarly, whereas the official poverty rate among children in female-headed families increased from 41.7% in 2008, to 43.4% in 2009, under a more comprehensive income definition, their poverty rate over the same period fell from 36.0% in 2008 to 32.1% in 2009 (see Figure 19).

The effects of congressional actions in response to the recent recession on poverty among single mothers and their children are especially telling under a more comprehensive income measure, but largely go unnoticed using the official measure. Congressional action in response to the recent recession appears to have helped counteract the rise in official poverty, and in 2009, to have resulted in a decline in poverty under a more comprehensive income definition than that offered by the official poverty measure. As noted earlier (section entitled: "Policy Responses to Changing Economic Conditions"), Congress extended and increased Unemployment Insurance benefits, expanded EITC payments to families with three or more children, expanded ACTC payments to lower-income families by lowering the credit's refundable income limit, increased SNAP benefits, and provided economic stimulus and recovery payments to families and individuals. Among these actions, only the UI benefit expansions would be captured under the official poverty measure.

The increased benefits under SNAP, EITC, and the ACTC are a temporary response to the recession, as were economic stimulus and recovery payments families received. ARRA's SNAP benefit increase is expected to last through FY2013. Similarly, ARRA expanded the EITC for families with three or more children, and extended the ACTC to lower income families through tax year 2010. The Tax Relief, Unemployment Insurance Reauthorization, and Job Creation Act of 2010 (P.L. 111-312) extended ARRA's EITC and ACTC provisions through tax year 2012, at which time they are scheduled to expire. Under the Census Bureau's official income and poverty measures the effects of these provisions will go unnoticed.

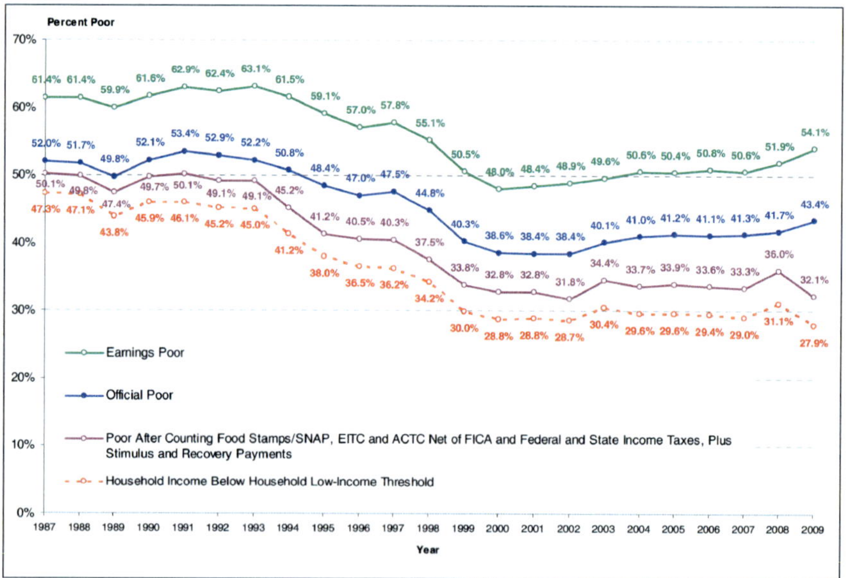

Source: Prepared by the Congressional Research Service (CRS) based on analysis of U.S. Census Bureau 1988 to 2010 Current Population Survey (CPS) Annual Social and Economic Supplement (ASEC) data. See Table C-15 for supporting data.

Figure 19. Poverty Among Children in Female-Headed Families Under Alternative Measures, 1987 to 2009.

A work-based income safety net depends upon a strong economy and available jobs for those who are able and willing to work. The EITC, as an earnings supplement, and the ACTC, as a family income supplement, are only available to working individuals. Work-based safety net programs may still help those who were without a job, for part of the year, or who have a job, but work fewer hours than they would like. However, as support programs, income from the EITC and ACTC are provided as a lump sum at the beginning of the year following that in which they were earned. As such, the EITC and ACTC may not help a family meet its immediate income needs due to job loss, or limited work hours. UI benefits are available only to those with an established work history and who lose a job for qualifying reasons. Work-based safety net benefits are of no use to individuals who have not recently held a job, and cannot find one.

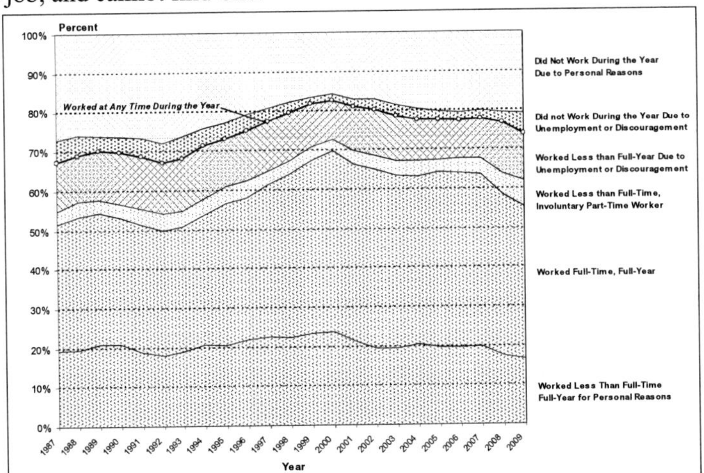

Source: Prepared by the Congressional Research Service (CRS) based on analysis of U.S. Census Bureau 1988 to 2010 Current Population Survey (CPS) Annual Social and Economic Supplement (ASEC) data. See Table C-17 for supporting data

Notes: Persons who worked for 50 weeks or more, and 35 or more hours per week, are designated as full-time, full-year workers. The unemployed are persons who were without a job and searched for work. Discouraged workers are persons who were without a job but did not search for work because they believed no jobs were available. Personal reasons for not working during the year, or working less than full-time, full-year, include taking care of a home or family, attending school, illness or disability, retired, or other.

Figure 20. Single Mothers' Job Attachment, 1987 to 2009.

Single Mothers' Attachment to the Work-Based Safety Net

With an increased share of single mothers engaged in the labor market since welfare reform, the availability of work, and especially full-time work for those who want it, is of special concern, given the recent recession and slow pace of recovery. Full-time, full-year work among single mothers peaked in 2000, and has fallen twice since, in response to two recessions (2000, and 2007-2009) (see Figure 20). A high-water mark was reached in 2000 when over four-fifths (83%) of single mothers had a job at some point during the year. By 2009, the share of single mothers with some attachment during the year had fallen to about three-quarters (74%). Comparing the two years, 46% worked full-time full-year in 2000, whereas only about two-fifths (39%) did so in 2009. The share of single mothers who were marginally employed during the year for economic reasons—they had a job at some time during the year, but for fewer hours or weeks than they desired—has risen from 13% of all single mothers in 2000, to 19% in 2009. Among this group are those who were unemployed (i.e., without a job for part of the year and looked for work) as well as "discouraged" workers (i.e., those who were without a job for part of the year and did not look for work because they believed no jobs were available); it also includes mothers who worked less than full-time, but desired full-time work.

In 2009, 74% of single mothers had some attachment to a job, and thus potentially had some connection to the work-based safety net. All of these mothers—those who worked full-time full-year, those who were marginally employed for economic reasons, and mothers who worked less than full-time full-year for personal reasons (i.e., taking care of home or family, going to school, ill or disabled, or retired/other)—might potentially benefit from the EITC, or the ACTC, depending on their annual earnings. Among those who worked for part of the year, but experienced a period of unemployment, some might qualify for UI benefits, depending on their work history and the conditions under which they separated from a job. In addition to the 74% of mothers with some job attachment, another 5% of single mothers were unemployed for the entire year, or without a job and did not work because they believed no work was available. Some of these mothers might also qualify for UI benefits depending on their circumstances.

Role of Traditional Welfare

Absent available jobs, single mothers may turn to the traditional cash welfare system (i.e., TANF), food assistance (SNAP), relatives and friends, for basic income support. In part contingent on the nature and pace of economic recovery, and federal and state budget pressures, funding for traditional welfare programs, as well as their structure[63] (e.g., time limits, work/participation requirements, education and training, and subsidized employment) may face increased attention, especially if the numbers of aid applicants increase given a dearth of jobs, and consequent lack of coverage under work-related safety net programs.

APPENDIX A. FROM MOTHERS' PENSIONS TO TANF – A BRIEF HISTORY

TANF, signed into law in 1996 as part of the Personal Responsibility and Work Opportunity Reconciliation Act (PRWORA) (P.L. 104-193), replaced the 61-year-old Aid to Families with Dependent Children (AFDC) program, a federal entitlement program to low-income families with children. The precursor program which TANF replaced, AFDC, had its beginnings in the Aid to Dependent Children (ADC) program, part of the 1935 Social Security Act, which introduced federal involvement in helping provide financial aid, or "public assistance," to aid dependent children.

Mothers' Pensions to Aid to Dependent Children[64]

Since at least the first White House Conference on Children in 1909 (Conference on the Care of Dependent Children), and the subsequent creation of the Children's Bureau in 1912, the federal government has been concerned with social conditions of children. The Conference was an impetus for states' enactment of state or locally financed mothers' pensions (also referred to as widows' pensions and or mothers' aid), which provided minimal cash support to mothers made destitute, usually due to a husband's death. Mothers' aid was intended to help keep mothers at home to supervise and care for their children, as an alternative to sending children to orphanages and/or putting them up for adoption, which was a common practice of the time.[65] Mothers' pensions largely went to widows, and payments were limited and restrictive (e.g., many states imposed rigid requirements as to the "character" of parents to assure that the child was living in a "suitable home" before granting aid; mothers were required to prove destitution,[66] and to agree to cease or limit employment upon receipt of a pension[67]). Prior to the 1935 Act, most states had adopted mothers' pension laws.[68]

As part of the Social Security Act of 1935, the federal Aid to Dependent Children (ADC) program introduced federal involvement in helping provide financial aid, or "public assistance," to aid dependent children. The ADC program essentially provided federal dollars to help support states mothers' pension programs, that nearly all states had established. Under the 1935 Act, a "dependent child" was defined as "a child under the age of sixteen who has been deprived of parental support or care by reason of the death, continued absence from the home, or physical or mental incapacity of a parent," and is living with one or more relatives in his or their own home.[69] The ADC program provided payments to states for aid to dependent children with approved state plans; federal payments at the time were one-third of the sums expended by the state up to a capped monthly expenditure amount per dependent child.[70] The federal program had no provision for assisting a parent or other relative in the household, although this changed over time.[71] In 1950, the federal government began to share in the maintenance costs of the parent or other caretaker relative. In 1962, support of a second parent in a family who was incapacitated or unemployed was allowed, and the program's name was changed to the Aid to Families with Dependent Children (AFDC).

Under state administration, ADC, as well as the mothers' pension programs which preceded it, favored children of widows over others. Early evidence from the program indicated that over half of all children assisted were dependent because of the death of a parent, with most living with their widowed mother; most of the remainder were living with mothers who were "deserted, divorced, or separated," or were living in other settings in which the mother was not present; about 2% were living with an unmarried mother.[72] The comparatively small share of unmarried mothers receiving ADC assistance in part reflected a program preference to serve widows, and some unmarried mothers were denied assistance by failing to meet "suitable home requirements." However, children of unmarried mothers at the time represented a relatively small share of all fatherless children in the early years of the ADC program. In 1938, children of unwed mothers represented an estimated 3.8% of all children in female-headed households in the U.S.[73] Social Security Act Amendments of 1939, extending Social Security benefits to widows and surviving children of deceased workers covered by the program, would have the effect of reducing the number of widows and their children from needing ADC, resulting in the program coming to primarily serve families in which fathers were absent due to divorce or abandonment. By

1961, widowed families would comprise only 7.7 percent of the ADC caseload, down from 43 percent in 1937.[74]

Increased Federal Involvement

In 1938, three years after enactment of the ADC, eight states were still not participating in the program.[75] In 1939, the federal payment rate was raised from one-third to one-half of a raised maximum payment amount per child, effective January 1940. With increasing federal dollars, the federal government would help assure state participation in the program, while at the same time gaining greater leverage in influencing the provision of assistance at the state level.[76] By June 1940, all states, the District of Columbia, Alaska, Hawaii, and Puerto Rico were participating in programs providing child welfare services under the Social Security Act.[77] Over time, the federal share of AFDC expenditures would increase, reaching a minimum of 50% and a permitted maximum of 83% of total AFDC expenditures by 1965, effective January 1966, for states with an approved plan for medical assistance programs under Title IXX of the Social Security Act (i.e., Medicaid).[78]

In 1961, the federal Bureau of Public Assistance (BPA), which ran the ADC program, issued a directive against states' and localities' use of "suitable home" rules, that had traditionally been used to keep children of unwed mothers out of the program. In 1966, the Bureau of Family Services, which had replaced the BPA in 1962, ordered that state plans for determining eligibility for AFDC "respect the rights of individuals ... .and not result in practices that violate the individual's privacy or personal dignity, or harass him, or violate his constitutional rights." Implicitly, states that did not comply could risk losing federal matching funds.[79]

Legal Challenges to Restrictive State Welfare Practices

Greater federal involvement and regulation of AFDC gave petitioners greater legal standing in federal court to challenge restrictive state welfare policies. While AFDC was an entitlement to eligible individuals, as defined by federal law, states still retained control in administering the program, which included determining eligibility of families applying for assistance. Although AFDC was an entitlement, practices of granting eligibility for the program varied widely among states and localities, as had been the case under the mothers' pensions in the pre-ADC era. The Economic Opportunity Act of 1964 (P.L. 88-452), the centerpiece of President Lyndon Johnson's "War on Poverty," focused national attention and federal assistance in helping to combat poverty. Among its provisions was the establishment of an Office of Economic Opportunity (OEO), which administered a number of programs under the act. Community Action Programs (CAP) were among OEO's programs, under which Community Action Agencies (CAAs) took root in local communities to help promote "maximum feasible participation" of the poor, intended to engage the poor in seeking solutions to poverty in their communities. OEO also set up legal services to aid the poor in local communities. At the same time, a burgeoning National Welfare Rights Organization (NWRO), independently began to advocate for the rights of the poor.[80] Growing political empowerment of the poor, combined with legal advocacy helped to overturn a number of restrictive state welfare policies by the U.S. Supreme Court. Such policies included "man-in-the-house" rules (King v. Smith, 392 U.S. 309 (1968)); long-term residency requirements (Shapiro v. Thompson, 394 U.S. 618 (1969)), and termination of assistance without a fair hearing (Goldberg v. Kelly, 397 U.S. 254 (1970)), among others. By one estimate, elimination of the residency requirements alone added some 800,000 persons to the AFDC rolls by 1970.[81]

Federal Efforts to Stem Rising Public Assistance Caseloads

Figure 2 depicts the number of recipients (children and adults) and welfare cases receiving assistance under AFDC (and ADC) from 1960 to 1994, the eve of the programs' repeal. While some federal efforts served to expand assistance caseloads, such as regulations and enforcement activities to promote states' administration of the program's individual entitlement provisions, and increasing federal matching payments to states, which shifted more of the financial burden of providing assistance from states to the federal government, other efforts would seek to restrain caseload growth and its underlying causes.

Expanding welfare caseloads were beginning to contribute to what some would refer to as a "welfare crisis," by the mid-1960s.[82] Contributing to the "crisis" was a *growing number of families potentially eligible* for cash assistance, as the baby-boom generation began entering adulthood, as well as changing social behavior relating to marriage, divorce, and childbearing. As noted earlier, in 1961 families headed by widowed mothers accounted for only about 8% of ADC families; from 1961 to 1967, the share of families receiving

AFDC who were headed by never-married mothers would increase from 21% to 28%.[83] In addition to an increasing number of *potentially* eligible families, an increasing share of such families applied for and were granted assistance during the 1960s, with the *participation of eligible families* in AFDC increasing "from perhaps 33 percent in the early 1960s to more than 90 percent in 1971.[84]"

The Rise (and Fall) of Social Services as an Answer to Reducing Welfare Dependency

The 1939 extension of social benefits to widows and surviving children of deceased covered workers had the effect of reducing the number of widows and their children needing assistance under ADC, resulting in the program coming to primarily serve families in which fathers were absent due to divorce or abandonment. Changing social trends regarding marriage, divorce, and childbearing in the post World War II era, contributed to the ADC program's growth. Under 1956 amendments to the Social Security Act (P.L. 84-880), Congress permitted federal funding to reimburse states for 50% of the costs of providing social services to public assistance recipients. Among the legislation's stated purpose was to enable states to "furnish financial assistance and other services ... to needy dependent children and the parents or relatives with whom they are living to help maintain and strengthen family life and ... attain the maximum level of self-support and personal independence."

Under 1962 amendments, funding for social services was expanded, and the federal matching rate was increased to 75%. Expanded funds for social services and training of skilled welfare workers marked the advent of the "casework approach" for addressing the multiple problems that many public assistance recipients faced. In his statement at the signing of the 1962 Amendments, President Kennedy described it as "a new approach-stressing services in addition to support, rehabilitation instead of relief, and training for useful work instead of prolonged dependency ... [the] objective is to prevent or reduce dependency and to encourage self-care and self-support to maintain family life where it is adequate and to restore it where it is deficient."[85]

Increased case supervision by social workers was intended to identify and address problems aid recipients faced, leading to their "rehabilitation" and helping to move them toward self sufficiency. A major premise was that the provision of social servicers could break the bonds of dependency many welfare families faced, by addressing their underlying problems. Consequent to the increased emphasis on social services, income maintenance workers often came to serve the dual function of eligibility technician and social caseworker. In implementing the law, the Department of Health, Education, and Welfare (HEW), set caseload and supervisory standards to assure smaller workloads and time for workers to deal with clients.[86] The amendments also provided additional funds for training welfare personnel in assuming the additional casework functions associated with identifying clients' need for services, as well as brokering and/or providing those services. Provision of social services became an integrated function with the provision of cash aid. States provided a panoply of services within a broad, somewhat ill-defined, range of service categories (e.g., educational or vocational training, health care, improved financial functioning, maintaining family life and improving family functioning, maintaining and improving social relationships and community life, self-care services, self-support services). In order to receive reimbursement at the 75% federal matching rate, a case had to be considered a "service case" and had to be part of a caseload of designated size. States faced a financial incentive to provide social services as a result of the comparatively high federal matching rate, which contributed to burgeoning federal spending on social services in the early 1970s.[87]

AFDC caseloads continued to rise through the course of the 1960s, in spite of increased funding for the provision of rehabilitative services. In 1972, HEW issued a mandate to states to separate the provision of services from the administrative function of determining eligibility for aid.[88] Under the mandate, social services would still be provided at the families' request, rather than on a routine basis. The 1974 Social Security Amendments created a new Title XX, which expanded eligibility for free or subsidized social services to the non-poor, but with a spending cap, rather than an open-ended matching grant. Title XX further severed the provision of social services from the provision of cash aid.

Federal Efforts to Constrain AFDC Caseload Growth due to Absent Fathers

Under 1967 Social Security Act amendments, Congress attempted to restrain AFDC caseload growth resulting from children's fathers continued absence from the home. States were required to establish programs to determine paternity and to locate absent parents and secure support from them.[89] Additionally, Congress imposed a "freeze" on federal matching payments for AFDC, which would limit the availability of federal matching funds for children who were receiving AFDC due to continued absence of a parent from the home.[90] Under the provision, federal matching funds would not be available to states after July 1, 1969 for any increase above the January-March 1968 level in the proportion of the state's children under age 18 receiving AFDC on grounds of the continued absence of their father. Implementation of the provision was postponed, and subsequently repealed by Congress in 1969 before taking effect (P.L. 91-41).

Under 1974 amendments to the Social Security Act, a new part D[91], Child Support and Establishment of Paternity, was added to title IV. Among Part D provisions, states were required to have plans for establishing paternity and establishing child support and were subject to loss of 5% of AFDC federal matching funds for failure to have "effective" programs. AFDC applicants and recipients were required to "cooperate" in identifying and locating children's fathers, and were required to assign child support rights to the state. Additionally, Part D required the Department of Health, Education, and Welfare (HEW) to establish a separate organizational unit to monitor state programs and to operate a Parent Locator Service, making use of federal and state records.[92]

Promoting Self-Sufficiency - Work Incentives, Requirements, and Sanctions

In 1961, Congress permitted states to include a second, unemployed, parent as part of the assistance unit under AFDC, the Unemployed Parent (AFDC-UP) program, but were required to deny assistance if the unemployed parent refused to accept work without "good cause".[93] In 1962, Congress authorized federal funds for states to establish Community Work and Training (CWT) programs for federally aided adult recipients. CWT jobs were to pay at least an equivalent wage for the same type of work as prevailing in the community, or the minimum wage, if higher. States were required to deduct only "net" earnings from the grant of the working welfare recipient (i.e., after any reasonable work-related expenses) and were permitted to allow working welfare recipients to deduct any income set aside for identifiable needs of the dependent child.[94]

Amendments of 1967 replaced CWT with the Work Incentive (WIN) program, a joint program between HEW and the Department of Labor (DOL), that required states to set up work and training programs for "appropriate" AFDC recipients.[95] The federal share of WIN spending was set at 80%, with states assuming the remainder. The 1967 amendments also required states to disregard a portion of AFDC adults' earnings—the first $30 plus one-third of the remainder—from income counted against the AFDC grant. Under prior law, other than a required deduction for work expenses from net earnings, the AFDC grant could be reduced by one dollar for every dollar earned. Under the 1967 provisions, the AFDC benefit would phase out more gradually, with a benefit reduction of 67 cents for each dollar earned during the month, in excess of $30. While providing a financial incentive for AFDC recipients to engage in work, the higher disregard would allow working recipients to stay on the program at higher income levels than otherwise, tending to have a potential countervailing influence on caseloads.

The 1967 amendments also signaled a shift in emphasis in the provision of services from "rehabilitative," personal "competence-enhancing," services, to work-related services, such as vocational training, job and work training referral, and child care, to promote self-sufficiency.[96]

In 1971, Congress required that all AFDC parents register for work or training, except for mothers with a child under age 6. In 1981, Congress gave states the authority to design and test their own "welfare-to-work" programs. In 1988, the Family Support Act replaced the WIN program with the Job Opportunities and Basic Skills Training program (JOBS). The program extended work requirements (which could include work preparation activities, such as education and training) from mothers with a child as young as six to mothers with a child as young as three and, at states' option, of extending work requirements to mothers with a child as young as age one. The act also required states to provide benefits to a second parent who was incapacitated or unemployed (AFDC-UP program).

A number of states experimented with changes to welfare policy under waiver authority granted to the Secretary of the Department of Health and Human Services (DHHS).[97] Among the features of state programs tested under waiver authority were efforts to strengthen work requirements, experiments requiring a "work first" approach rather than "training first, followed by work," time limits, strengthened sanctions for noncompliance with welfare rules, and capping of welfare benefits for a new baby conceived or born while a mother was receiving welfare.

APPENDIX B. CASH WELFARE UNDER-REPORTING ON THE CPS

A comparison of AFDC/TANF administrative statistics and CPS-estimated caseload counts suggests that the CPS undercounts actual cases and that the CPS undercount has worsened in recent years. Figure B-1 shows that from 1987 to 1991, the CPS accounted for roughly 80% of the AFDC administrative caseload count, but in 2006 the CPS captured only about 55%.[98] Worsened reporting of cash welfare on the CPS makes it difficult to gauge how much of the drop in welfare receipt among single mothers represents eligible families who do not receive assistance, rather than families who do not report actual welfare aid on the CPS.

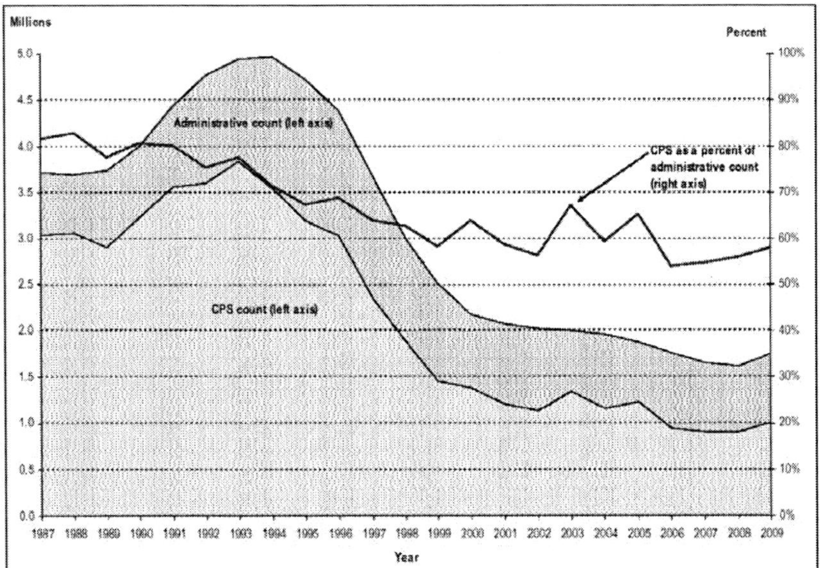

Source: Prepared by the Congressional Research Service (CRS) based on analysis of U.S. Census Bureau 1988 to 2010 Current Population Survey (CPS) Annual Social and Economic Supplement (ASEC) data and Department of Health and Human Services (DHHS) caseload data. See Table B-1 for supporting data.

Figure B-1. AFDC/TANF Cases: CPS Estimates Versus Administrative Caseload Counts (Annual Monthly Average), 1987 to 2009.

Table B-1. AFDC/TANF Cases: CPS Versus Administrative Caseload Counts, Annual Monthly Average, 1987 to 2009 (Numbers in millions)

Year	Persons Reporting AFDC or TANF Receipt on the CPS[a]	AFDC and TANF cases Based on Administrative Data[b]	CPS as a Percent of Administrative Total
1987	3.039	3.719	81.7%
1988	3.056	3.691	82.8%
1989	2.901	3.738	77.6%
1990	3.226	3.995	80.8%
1991	3.554	4.434	80.2%
1992	3.596	4.765	75.5%
1993	3.844	4.949	77.7%
1994	3.551	4.972	71.4%
1995	3.193	4.734	67.8%
1996	3.022	4.380	69.0%
1997	2.355	3.690	63.8%
1998	1.892	3.007	62.9%
1999	1.464	2.515	58.2%
2000	1.392	2.181	63.8%
2001	1.216	2.075	58.6%
2002	1.140	2.023	56.3%
2003	1.346	2.001	67.3%
2004	1.160	1.958	59.3%
2005	1.227	1.876	65.4%
2006	0.955	1.766	54.1%
2007	0.907	1.659	54.7%
2008	0.905	1.620	55.9%
2009	1.017	1.755	57.9%

Source: Congressional Research Service (CRS) estimates based on U.S. Bureau of the Census 1988 to 2010 Current Population Survey (CPS) Annual Social and Economic Supplement (ASEC) data and U.S. Department of Health and Human Services (DHHS) AFDC and TANF caseload data.

Note: Support table for Figure B-1.

a. Estimated average monthly number based on number of months CPS respondents indicated they received AFDC or TANF during the year.

b. Average monthly number of AFDC or TANF cases in the 50 states and the District of Columbia.

APPENDIX C. SUPPORT TABLES

Table C-1. Children's Family Living Arrangements and Poverty Status, 1987 to 2009 (Numbers in 1,000s)

Year	Total	Married -Couple Families	Female-Headed Families					Male-Headed Families, Spouse Absent	Lives with Other Relatives, Apart from Parents
			Total	Never Married	Separated, Spouse Absent	Divorced	Widowed		
All Children—Numbers in 1,000s									
1987	62,906	46,062	13,617	4,231	3,405	5,041	939	1,795	1,433
1988	63,398	46,562	13,700	4,290	3,380	5,227	803	1,795	1,341
1989	63,816	46,526	13,874	4,365	3,416	5,118	975	1,994	1,421
1990	64,730	46,674	14,608	5,040	3,583	5,206	780	2,022	1,426
1991	65,576	46,662	15,396	5,410	3,790	5,507	688	2,185	1,333
1992	66,511	47,197	15,586	5,511	3,739	5,687	649	2,287	1,441
1993	68,879	48,128	16,338	6,003	3,839	5,800	696	2,262	2,150
1994	69,596	48,300	16,480	5,865	3,901	6,019	695	2,467	2,350
1995	70,140	48,246	16,993	6,363	3,928	6,040	662	2,764	2,136
1996	70,194	48,412	16,740	6,596	3,753	5,824	566	3,061	1,981
1997	70,561	48,649	16,639	6,696	3,560	5,708	676	3,146	2,126
1998	70,864	48,805	16,833	6,759	3,561	5,828	685	3,098	2,129
1999	71,200	49,814	16,172	6,590	3,225	5,658	698	3,062	2,152
2000	71,261	49,820	16,120	6,734	3,109	5,577	699	3,137	2,184

Table C-1. (Continued)

Year	Total	Married -Couple Families	Female-Headed Families					Male-Headed Families, Spouse Absent	Lives with Other Relatives, Apart from Parents
			Total	Never Married	Separated, Spouse Absent	Divorced	Widowed		
2001	71,534	49,685	16,483	6,872	3,289	5,602	720	3,294	2,072
2002	72,238	49,925	16,780	7,008	3,351	5,758	663	3,321	2,211
2003	72,484	49,596	17,116	7,202	3,298	5,910	706	3,392	2,379
2004	72,757	49,499	17,229	7,428	3,395	5,809	597	3,500	2,528
2005	72,717	49,675	17,162	7,441	3,331	5,769	621	3,467	2,413
2006	73,259	49,992	17,921	7,833	3,616	5,876	596	3,327	2,018
2007	73,554	49,406	18,178	8,203	3,512	5,799	663	3,718	2,251
2008	73,637	49,583	18,086	8,394	3,688	5,367	637	3,614	2,355
2009	74,101	49,117	18,706	8,646	3,895	5,524	641	3,898	2,380
All Children—Percent Distribution									
1987	100.0%	73.2%	21.6%	6.7%	5.4%	8.0%	1.5%	2.9%	2.3%
1988	100.0%	73.4%	21.6%	6.8%	5.3%	8.2%	1.3%	2.8%	2.1%
1989	100.0%	72.9%	21.7%	6.8%	5.4%	8.0%	1.5%	3.1%	2.2%
1990	100.0%	72.1%	22.6%	7.8%	5.5%	8.0%	1.2%	3.1%	2.2%
1991	100.0%	71.2%	23.5%	8.3%	5.8%	8.4%	1.0%	3.3%	2.0%
1992	100.0%	71.0%	23.4%	8.3%	5.6%	8.6%	1.0%	3.4%	2.2%
-1993	100.0%	69.9%	23.7%	8.7%	5.6%	8.4%	1.0%	3.3%	3.1%
1994	100.0%	69.4%	23.7%	8.4%	5.6%	8.6%	1.0%	3.5%	3.4%

Year	Total	Married -Couple Families	Female-Headed Families					Male-Headed Families, Spouse Absent	Lives with Other Relatives, Apart from Parents
			Total	Never Married	Separated, Spouse Absent	Divorced	Widowed		
1995	100.0%	68.8%	24.2%	9.1%	5.6%	8.6%	0.9%	3.9%	3.0%
1996	100.0%	69.0%	23.8%	9.4%	5.3%	8.3%	0.8%	4.4%	2.8%
1997	100.0%	68.9%	23.6%	9.5%	5.0%	8.1%	1.0%	4.5%	3.0%
1998	100.0%	68.9%	23.8%	9.5%	5.0%	8.2%	1.0%	4.4%	3.0%
1999	100.0%	70.0%	22.7%	9.3%	4.5%	7.9%	1.0%	4.3%	3.0%
2000	100.0%	69.9%	22.6%	9.5%	4.4%	7.8%	1.0%	4.4%	3.1%
2001	100.0%	69.5%	23.0%	9.6%	4.6%	7.8%	1.0%	4.6%	2.9%
2002	100.0%	69.1%	23.2%	9.7%	4.6%	8.0%	0.9%	4.6%	3.1%
2003	100.0%	68.4%	23.6%	9.9%	4.5%	8.2%	1.0%	4.7%	3.3%
2004	100.0%	68.0%	23.7%	10.2%	4.7%	8.0%	0.8%	4.8%	3.5%
2005	100.0%	68.3%	23.6%	10.2%	4.6%	7.9%	0.9%	4.8%	3.3%
2006	100.0%	68.2%	24.5%	10.7%	4.9%	8.0%	0.8%	4.5%	2.8%
2007	100.0%	67.2%	24.7%	11.2%	4.8%	7.9%	0.9%	5.1%	3.1%
2008	100.0%	67.3%	24.6%	11.4%	5.0%	7.3%	0.9%	4.9%	3.2%
2009	100.0%	66.3%	25.2%	11.7%	5.3%	7.5%	0.9%	5.3%	3.2%
Poor Children—Numbers in 1,000s									
1987	12,580	4,619	7,081	2,845	2,106	1,801	329	332	549
1988	12,224	4,317	7,088	2,821	2,040	1,925	301	365	456
1989	12,380	4,535	6,904	2,800	1,879	1,856	369	416	524
1990	13,214	4,718	7,615	3,306	2,127	1,910	273	378	503

Table C-1. (Continued)

Year	Total	Married -Couple Families	Female-Headed Families					Male-Headed Families, Spouse Absent	Lives with Other Relatives, Apart from Parents
			Total	Never Married	Separated, Spouse Absent	Divorced	Widowed		
1991	14,054	4,869	8,223	3,578	2,439	2,016	191	469	493
1992	14,385	4,987	8,252	3,654	2,204	2,183	210	541	606
1993	15,456	5,571	8,532	3,869	2,230	2,178	255	546	807
1994	15,013	5,258	8,367	3,655	2,201	2,297	214	644	743
1995	14,345	4,763	8,221	4,015	2,140	1,875	191	606	755
1996	14,126	4,802	7,861	3,882	1,917	1,878	183	682	781
1997	13,786	4,503	7,907	3,870	1,814	2,034	188	628	749
1998	13,144	4,380	7,541	3,720	1,794	1,799	228	613	610
1999	11,812	4,100	6,515	3,437	1,346	1,532	200	558	639
2000	11,337	3,905	6,216	3,211	1,368	1,393	243	575	641
2001	11,450	3,896	6,334	3,233	1,326	1,540	236	634	585
2002	11,869	4,188	6,443	3,269	1,497	1,465	212	606	631
2003	12,591	4,218	6,868	3,631	1,444	1,588	205	775	729
2004	12,760	4,315	7,065	3,742	1,582	1,541	200	641	739
2005	12,582	4,104	7,077	3,819	1,597	1,492	169	645	756
2006	12,589	3,978	7,371	3,884	1,625	1,655	209	678	562
2007	13,114	4,125	7,511	4,111	1,593	1,577	231	765	714
2008	13,826	4,792	7,536	4,230	1,633	1,469	203	762	735

Year	Total	Married -Couple Families	Female-Headed Families					Male-Headed Families, Spouse Absent	Lives with Other Relatives, Apart from Parents
			Total	Never Married	Separated, Spouse Absent	Divorced	Widowed		
2009	15,168	5,355	8,113	4,482	1,826	1,613	192	1,063	637
Poor Children—Percentage Distribution									
1987	100.0%	36.7%	56.3%	22.6%	16.7%	14.3%	2.6%	2.6%	4.4%
1988	100.0%	35.3%	58.0%	23.1%	16.7%	15.7%	2.5%	3.0%	3.7%
1989	100.0%	36.6%	55.8%	22.6%	15.2%	15.0%	3.0%	3.4%	4.2%
1990	100.0%	35.7%	57.6%	25.0%	16.1%	14.5%	2.1%	2.9%	3.8%
1991	100.0%	34.6%	58.5%	25.5%	17.4%	14.3%	1.4%	3.3%	3.5%
1992	100.0%	34.7%	57.4%	25.4%	15.3%	15.2%	1.5%	3.8%	4.2%
1993	100.0%	36.0%	55.2%	25.0%	14.4%	14.1%	1.7%	3.5%	5.2%
1994	100.0%	35.0%	55.7%	24.3%	14.7%	15.3%	1.4%	4.3%	4.9%
1995	100.0%	33.2%	57.3%	28.0%	14.9%	13.1%	1.3%	4.2%	5.3%
1996	100.0%	34.0%	55.6%	27.5%	13.6%	13.3%	1.3%	4.8%	5.5%
1997	100.0%	32.7%	57.4%	28.1%	13.2%	14.8%	1.4%	4.6%	5.4%
1998	100.0%	33.3%	57.4%	28.3%	13.6%	13.7%	1.7%	4.7%	4.6%
1999	100.0%	34.7%	55.2%	29.1%	11.4%	13.0%	1.7%	4.7%	5.4%
2000	100.0%	34.4%	54.8%	28.3%	12.1%	12.3%	2.1%	5.1%	5.7%
2001	100.0%	34.0%	55.3%	28.2%	11.6%	13.4%	2.1%	5.5%	5.1%
2002	100.0%	35.3%	54.3%	27.5%	12.6%	12.3%	1.8%	5.1%	5.3%
2003	100.0%	33.5%	54.6%	28.8%	11.5%	12.6%	1.6%	6.2%	5.8%
2004	100.0%	33.8%	55.4%	29.3%	12.4%	12.1%	1.6%	5.0%	5.8%

Table C-1. (Continued)

Year	Total	Married -Couple Families	Female-Headed Families					Male-Headed Families, Spouse Absent	Lives with Other Relatives, Apart from Parents
			Total	Never Married	Separated, Spouse Absent	Divorced	Widowed		
2005	100.0%	32.6%	56.3%	30.4%	12.7%	11.9%	1.3%	5.1%	6.0%
2006	100.0%	31.6%	58.6%	30.9%	12.9%	13.1%	1.7%	5.4%	4.5%
2007	100.0%	31.5%	57.3%	31.3%	12.1%	12.0%	1.8%	5.8%	5.4%
2008	100.0%	34.7%	54.5%	30.6%	11.8%	10.6%	1.5%	5.5%	5.3%
2009	100.0%	35.3%	53.5%	29.5%	12.0%	10.6%	1.3%	7.0%	4.2%
Child Poverty Rate—Poor Children as a Percent of Total Children, By Family Living Arrangement									
1987	20.0%	10.0%	52.0%	67.2%	61.8%	35.7%	35.1%	18.5%	38.3%
1988	19.3%	9.3%	51.7%	65.7%	60.4%	36.8%	37.5%	20.3%	34.0%
1989	19.4%	9.7%	49.8%	64.1%	55.0%	36.3%	37.8%	20.9%	36.9%
1990	20.4%	10.1%	52.1%	65.6%	59.4%	36.7%	34.9%	18.7%	35.3%
1991	21.4%	10.4%	53.4%	66.1%	64.3%	36.6%	27.7%	21.5%	37.0%
1992	21.6%	10.6%	52.9%	66.3%	58.9%	38.4%	32.3%	23.6%	42.1%
1993	22.4%	11.6%	52.2%	64.4%	58.1%	37.5%	36.7%	24.1%	37.5%
1994	21.6%	10.9%	50.8%	62.3%	56.4%	38.2%	30.8%	26.1%	31.6%
1995	20.5%	9.9%	48.4%	63.1%	54.5%	31.0%	28.8%	21.9%	35.4%
1996	20.1%	9.9%	47.0%	58.8%	51.1%	32.2%	32.4%	22.3%	39.4%
1997	19.5%	9.3%	47.5%	57.8%	51.0%	35.6%	27.8%	20.0%	35.2%
1998	18.5%	9.0%	44.8%	55.0%	50.4%	30.9%	33.3%	19.8%	28.7%

Year	Total	Married -Couple Families	Female-Headed Families					Male-Headed Families, Spouse Absent	Lives with Other Relatives, Apart from Parents
			Total	Never Married	Separated, Spouse Absent	Divorced	Widowed		
1999	16.6%	8.2%	40.3%	52.2%	41.7%	27.1%	28.7%	18.2%	29.7%
2000	15.9%	7.8%	38.6%	47.7%	44.0%	25.0%	34.8%	18.3%	29.4%
2001	16.0%	7.8%	38.4%	47.0%	40.3%	27.5%	32.7%	19.3%	28.3%
2002	16.4%	8.4%	38.4%	46.6%	44.7%	25.5%	31.9%	18.3%	28.5%
2003	17.4%	8.5%	40.1%	50.4%	43.8%	26.9%	29.1%	22.8%	30.6%
2004	17.5%	8.7%	41.0%	50.4%	46.6%	26.5%	33.5%	18.3%	29.2%
2005	17.3%	8.3%	41.2%	51.3%	47.9%	25.9%	27.2%	18.6%	31.3%
2006	17.2%	8.0%	41.1%	49.6%	44.9%	28.2%	35.0%	20.4%	27.9%
2007	17.8%	8.3%	41.3%	50.1%	45.3%	27.2%	34.9%	20.6%	31.7%
2008	18.8%	9.7%	41.7%	50.4%	44.3%	27.4%	31.9%	21.1%	31.2%
2009	20.5%	10.9%	43.4%	51.8%	46.9%	29.2%	29.9%	27.3%	26.8%

Source: Congressional Research Service (CRS) estimates based on analysis of U.S. Census Bureau 1988 to 2010 Current Population Survey (CPS) Annual Social and Economic Supplement (ASEC) data.

Note: Support table for Figure 1.

Table C-2. Number of Recipients and Cases Receiving Assistance Under ADC, AFDC, and TANF, 1960 to 2010 (Annual monthly average, in millions)

Calendar Year	Cases	Recipients	Children	Adults
1960	790,910	3,011,508	2,330,042	691,956
1961	872,722	3,362,722	2,597,700	765,022
1962	939,275	3,703,896	2,843,652	860,244
1963	963,368	3,944,635	2,956,962	987,673
1964	1,010,107	4,194,603	3,144,690	1,049,913
1965	1,060,214	4,421,650	3,320,559	1,101,091
1966	1,095,533	4,546,122	3,433,908	1,112,215
1967	1,219,553	5,013,795	3,771,218	1,242,578
1968	1,409,664	5,702,377	4,273,606	1,428,771
1969	1,695,612	6,689,158	4,973,458	1,715,700
1970	2,206,799	8,461,892	6,211,583	2,250,308
1971	2,762,619	10,242,130	7,434,512	2,807,618
1972	3,048,031	10,944,008	7,905,071	3,038,937
1973	3,147,972	10,949,112	7,902,756	3,046,356
1974	3,187,232	10,825,730	7,803,440	3,022,291
1975	3,481,362	11,318,736	8,070,972	3,247,764
1976	3,564,887	11,283,516	7,981,688	3,301,829
1977	3,568,481	11,015,176	7,742,535	3,272,641
1978	3,516,649	10,550,607	7,363,099	3,187,509
1979	3,509,192	10,311,586	7,181,272	3,130,314
1980	3,712,309	10,774,046	7,419,183	3,354,864
1981	3,835,489	11,079,117	7,526,934	3,552,183
1982	3,541,525	10,358,302	6,902,830	3,455,472
1983	3,686,163	10,760,935	7,097,744	3,663,191
1984	3,713,929	10,830,529	7,143,705	3,686,824
1985	3,701,033	10,855,284	7,197,601	3,657,683
1986	3,763,252	11,037,797	7,333,801	3,703,996

Calendar Year	Cases	Recipients	Children	Adults
1987	3,775,573	11,026,664	7,366,159	3,660,505
1988	3,748,580	10,914,679	7,328,786	3,585,893
1989	3,798,348	10,992,248	7,418,966	3,573,282
1990	4,056,584	11,694,712	7,910,836	3,783,876
1991	4,497,186	12,930,472	8,714,749	4,215,723
1992	4,829,094	13,773,319	9,302,846	4,470,473
1993	5,011,827	14,205,484	9,574,475	4,631,010
1994	5,032,632	14,160,920	9,568,359	4,592,561
1995	4,790,749	13,418,386	9,134,603	4,283,783
1996	4,434,160	12,320,970	8,468,759	3,852,212
1997	3,740,179	10,375,993	n/a	n/a
1998	3,050,335	8,347,136	n/a	n/a
1999	2,554,069	6,824,347	n/a	n/a
2000	2,302,780	6,143,156	4,478,742	1,654,818
2001	2,191,506	5,716,797	4,200,666	1,515,552
2002	2,187,158	5,609,012	4,118,797	1,479,433
2003	2,180,075	5,489,786	4,062,665	1,416,022
2004	2,153,066	5,341,859	3,969,376	1,361,701
2005	2,060,282	5,025,650	3,758,077	1,261,392
2006	1,905,785	4,577,114	3,455,961	1,121,153
2007	1,729,894	4,075,611	3,119,519	956,091
2008	1,700,249	4,001,330	3,056,690	944,640
2009	1,838,169	4,367,414	3,294,392	1,073,254
2010[a]	1,909,275	4,569,433	3,418,995	1,150,438

Source: Figure prepared by the Congressional Research Service (CRS) from Department of Health and Human Services (DHHS), Office of Family Assistance (OFA), available at http://www.acf.hhs.gov/programs/ofa/data-reports/index.htm.

Notes: N/A separate estimates for children and adults are not available from 1997 to 1999, due to changes in state reporting requirements during the transition from AFDC to TANF.

Support table for Figure 2 and Figure 3.

a. Preliminary data based on the first nine months of 2010.

Table C-3. Poverty Among Related Children Under Age 18, All Children and Children in Female-Headed Households (No Spouse Present) 1960 to 2009 (Numbers in 1,000s)

Year	All Children			Children in Female-Headed Households				
	Total	Poor	Poverty Rate (percent poor)	Total	Share of all Children	Poor	Share of all Poor Children	Poverty Rate (percent poor)
1960	65,275	17,288	26.5	5,987	9.2	4,095	23.7	68.4
1961	65,792	16,577	25.2	6,212	9.4	4,044	24.4	65.1
1962	67,385	16,630	24.7	6,419	9.5	4,506	27.1	70.2
1963	68,837	15,691	22.8	6,419	9.3	4,554	29.0	70.9
1964	69,364	15,736	22.7	6,838	9.9	4,422	28.1	64.7
1965	69,638	14,388	20.7	7,098	10.2	4,562	31.7	64.3
1966	69,869	12,146	17.4	7,106	10.2	4,262	35.1	60.0
1967	70,058	11,427	16.3	7,344	10.5	4,246	37.2	57.8
1968	70,035	10,739	15.3	7,323	10.5	4,409	41.1	60.2
1969	68,746	9,501	13.8	7,820	11.4	4,247	44.7	54.3
1970	68,815	10,235	14.9	7,987	11.6	4,689	45.8	58.7
1971	68,474	10,344	15.1	9,127	13.3	4,850	46.9	53.1
1972	67,592	10,082	14.9	9,600	14.2	5,094	50.5	53.1
1973	66,626	9,453	14.2	9,929	14.9	5,171	54.7	52.1
1974	65,802	9,967	15.1	10,458	15.9	5,387	54.0	51.5
1975	64,750	10,882	16.8	10,622	16.4	5,597	51.4	52.7
1976	63,729	10,081	15.8	10,739	16.9	5,583	55.4	52.0
1977	62,823	10,028	16.0	11,238	17.9	5,658	56.4	50.3
1978	61,987	9,722	15.7	11,232	18.1	5,687	58.5	50.6
1979	62,646	9,993	16.0	11,595	18.5	5,635	56.4	48.6
1980	62,168	11,114	17.9	11,539	18.6	5,866	52.8	50.8
1981	61,756	12,068	19.5	12,059	19.5	6,305	52.2	52.3
1982	61,565	13,139	21.3	11,946	19.4	6,696	51.0	56.1
1983	61,578	13,427	21.8	12,172	19.8	6,747	50.2	55.4
1984	61,681	12,929	21.0	12,536	20.3	6,772	52.4	54.0
1985	62,019	12,483	20.1	12,531	20.2	6,716	53.8	53.6
1986	62,009	12,257	19.8	12,763	20.6	6,943	56.6	54.4

Year	All Children			Children in Female-Headed Households				
	Total	Poor	Poverty Rate (percent poor)	Total	Share of all Children	Poor	Share of all Poor Children	Poverty Rate (percent poor)
1987	62,423	12,275	19.7	13,066	20.9	7,019	57.2	53.7
1988	62,906	11,935	19.0	13,146	20.9	6,955	58.3	52.9
1989	63,225	12,001	19.0	13,316	21.1	6,808	56.7	51.1
1990	63,908	12,715	19.9	13,793	21.6	7,363	57.9	53.4
1991	64,800	13,658	21.1	14,545	22.4	8,065	59.0	55.4
1992	67,256	14,521	21.6	15,319	22.8	8,368	57.6	54.6
1993	68,040	14,961	22.0	15,844	23.3	8,503	56.8	53.7
1994	68,819	14,610	21.2	15,924	23.1	8,427	57.7	52.9
1995	69,425	13,999	20.2	16,637	24.0	8,364	59.7	50.3
1996	69,411	13,764	19.8	16,213	23.4	7,990	58.0	49.3
1997	69,844	13,422	19.2	16,175	23.2	7,928	59.1	49.0
1998	70,253	12,845	18.3	16,550	23.6	7,627	59.4	46.1
1999	70,424	11,678	16.6	15,891	22.6	6,694	57.3	42.1
2000	70,538	11,005	15.6	15,717	22.3	6,300	57.2	40.1
2001	70,950	11,175	15.8	16,137	22.7	6,341	56.7	39.3
2002	71,619	11,646	16.3	16,565	23.1	6,564	56.4	39.6
2003	71,907	12,340	17.2	16,964	23.6	7,085	57.4	41.8
2004	72,133	12,473	17.3	17,081	23.7	7,152	57.3	41.9
2005	72,095	12,335	17.1	16,862	23.4	7,210	58.4	42.8
2006	72,609	12,299	16.9	17,416	24.0	7,341	59.7	42.2
2007	72,792	12,802	17.6	17,557	24.1	7,546	58.9	43.0
2008	72,980	13,507	18.5	17,456	23.9	7,587	56.2	43.5
2009	73,410	14,774	20.1	17,907	24.4	7,942	53.8	44.4

Source: Prepared by the Congressional Research Service (CRS) based on U.S. Census Bureau historical series, available at http://www.census.gov/hhes/www/poverty data/historical/people.html, "Table 10. Related Children in Female Householder Families, by Poverty Status."

Notes: Estimates are for children in female-headed "households," which differs somewhat from the CRS definition of female-headed "families" used later in this report based on analysis of U.S. Census Bureau Current Population Survey (CPS) Annual Social and Economic Supplement (ASEC) data.

Support table for Figure 4.

Table C-4. Mothers with Related Children Under Age 18, by Poverty and Marital Status, 1987 to 2009 (in thousands)

Year	Single Mothers																	
	All Single Mothers			Never Married			Separated, Spouse Absent			Divorced			Widowed			Married, Spouse Present		
	Total	Poor	Pct. Poor	Total	Poor	Pct. Poor	Total	Poor	Pct. Poor	Total	Poor	Pct. Poor	Total	Poor	Pct. Poor	Total	Poor	Pct. Poor
1987	8,193	3,661	44.7%	2,689	1,559	58.0%	1,787	975	54.6%	3,130	948	30.3%	588	180	30.6%	24,992	1,912	7.7%
1988	8,321	3,650	43.9%	2,798	1,595	57.0%	1,770	911	51.5%	3,224	966	30.0%	529	177	33.5%	25,096	1,785	7.1%
1989	8,400	3,506	41.7%	2,775	1,536	55.4%	1,836	860	46.9%	3,197	930	29.1%	593	179	30.2%	24,921	1,816	7.3%
1990	8,745	3,821	43.7%	3,100	1,730	55.8%	1,922	986	51.3%	3,225	956	29.6%	498	148	29.7%	24,863	1,938	7.8%
1991	9,031	4,101	45.4%	3,284	1,909	58.1%	1,950	1,075	55.1%	3,349	1,017	30.4%	448	99	22.2%	24,880	2,075	8.3%
1992	9,567	4,339	45.4%	3,595	2,059	57.3%	2,027	1,039	51.3%	3,524	1,128	32.0%	421	112	26.6%	25,386	2,178	8.6%
1993	9,860	4,456	45.2%	3,830	2,139	55.8%	2,044	1,050	51.4%	3,544	1,128	31.8%	443	140	31.7%	25,614	2,295	9.0%
1994	9,837	4,203	42.7%	3,681	1,982	53.8%	2,050	992	48.4%	3,674	1,113	30.3%	432	117	27.0%	25,646	2,170	8.5%
1995	9,887	3,971	40.2%	3,724	1,963	52.7%	2,083	960	46.1%	3,668	949	25.9%	411	99	24.0%	25,386	1,923	7.6%
1996	10,052	4,005	39.8%	4,097	2,033	49.6%	1,965	869	44.3%	3,605	988	27.4%	385	115	29.9%	25,603	1,921	7.5%
1997	9,874	3,946	40.0%	4,154	2,043	49.2%	1,838	794	43.2%	3,448	1,014	29.4%	435	95	21.8%	25,735	1,785	6.9%
1998	9,881	3,685	37.3%	4,184	1,933	46.2%	1,813	754	41.6%	3,489	884	25.3%	396	115	29.1%	25,573	1,775	6.9%
1999	9,741	3,314	34.0%	4,197	1,869	44.5%	1,725	598	34.6%	3,425	750	21.9%	394	98	24.8%	25,806	1,647	6.4%
2000	9,712	3,090	31.8%	4,199	1,668	39.7%	1,662	610	36.7%	3,404	696	20.5%	447	116	26.0%	26,563	1,557	5.9%
2001	10,044	3,259	32.4%	4,311	1,716	39.8%	1,787	614	34.4%	3,501	804	23.0%	445	124	27.9%	26,303	1,574	6.0%
2002	10,206	3,284	32.2%	4,422	1,737	39.3%	1,822	695	38.2%	3,538	736	20.8%	424	115	27.2%	26,484	1,789	6.8%
2003	10,411	3,525	33.9%	4,511	1,917	42.5%	1,758	650	37.0%	3,699	847	22.9%	443	110	24.8%	26,414	1,841	7.0%
2004	10,489	3,663	34.9%	4,647	2,016	43.4%	1,806	726	40.2%	3,631	810	22.3%	404	111	27.4%	26,797	1,858	6.9%
2005	10,476	3,640	34.7%	4,657	2,040	43.8%	1,777	716	40.3%	3,618	786	21.7%	424	98	23.1%	26,507	1,729	6.5%

Year	Single Mothers																	
	All Single Mothers			Never Married			Separated, Spouse Absent			Divorced			Widowed			Married, Spouse Present		
	Total	Poor	Pct. Poor	Total	Poor	Pct. Poor	Total	Poor	Pct. Poor	Total	Poor	Pct. Poor	Total	Poor	Pct. Poor	Total	Poor	Pct. Poor
2006	10,938	3,841	35.1%	4,934	2,100	42.6%	1,970	777	39.5%	3,652	850	23.3%	381	114	29.9%	26,857	1,709	6.4%
2007	10,748	3,790	35.3%	4,961	2,135	43.0%	1,873	734	39.2%	3,507	796	22.7%	407	124	30.6%	25,851	1,718	6.6%
2008	10,797	3,863	35.8%	5,120	2,220	43.4%	2,002	772	38.5%	3,284	759	23.1%	391	112	28.6%	25,861	1,933	7.5%
2009	10,990	4,128	37.6%	5,225	2,365	45.3%	2,019	825	40.8%	3,333	831	24.9%	413	107	26.0%	25,398	2,109	8.3%

Source: Congressional Research Service (CRS) estimates based on analysis of U.S. Census Bureau 1988 to 2010 Current Population Survey (CPS) Annual Social and Economic Supplement (ASEC) data.

Note: Support table for Figure 5 and Figure 6.

Table C-5. Single Mothers: Poverty and Cash Welfare Receipt, 1987 to 2009 (in thousands)

Year	Number of Mother-Only Families	Number Receiving AFDC/TANF	Poor but Not Receiving AFDC/TANF	Neither Poor nor Receiving AFDC/TANF
1987	8,193	2,719	1,399	4,076
1988	8,321	2,737	1,380	4,204
1989	8,400	2,537	1,452	4,411
1990	8,745	2,901	1,456	4,387
1991	9,031	3,101	1,554	4,375
1992	9,567	3,300	1,691	4,575
1993	9,860	3,439	1,722	4,700
1994	9,837	3,166	1,754	4,916
1995	9,887	2,862	1,818	5,207
1996	10,052	2,669	1,946	5,437
1997	9,874	2,225	2,211	5,438
1998	9,881	1,872	2,253	5,756
1999	9,741	1,543	2,216	5,981
2000	9,712	1,215	2,251	6,246
2001	10,044	1,064	2,501	6,479
2002	10,206	1,025	2,577	6,604
2003	10,411	1,253	2,610	6,448
2004	10,442	1,054	2,890	6,498
2005	10,476	1,102	2,837	6,537
2006	10,938	991	3,120	6,827
2007	10,748	878	3,142	6,728
2008	10,797	974	3,161	6,662
2009	10,990	967	3,408	6,615

Source: Congressional Research Service (CRS) estimates based on analysis of U.S. Census Bureau 1988 to 2010 Current Population Survey (CPS) Annual Social and Economic Supplement (ASEC) data.

Note: Support table for Figure 7.

Table C-6. Welfare, Work, and Poverty Status Among Single Mothers, 1987 to 2009

Year	Percent who Worked During Year	Percent Poor ("official definition")	Percent who Received AFDC/TANF During the Year		
			Total	Did not Work During Year	Worked During Year
1987	67.3%	44.7%	33.2%	21.8%	11.4%
1988	68.9%	43.9%	32.9%	21.1%	11.8%
1989	70.1%	41.7%	30.2%	20.1%	10.1%
1990	69.8%	43.7%	33.2%	20.9%	12.3%
1991	68.7%	45.4%	34.3%	22.0%	12.3%
1992	67.2%	45.4%	34.5%	22.2%	12.3%
1993	68.1%	45.2%	34.9%	21.8%	13.1%
1994	71.4%	42.7%	32.2%	18.8%	13.4%
1995	73.0%	40.2%	28.9%	16.5%	12.4%
1996	75.1%	39.8%	26.65	14.6%	12.0%
1997	77.3%	40.0%	22.5%	11.4%	11.1%
1998	79.6%	37.3%	18.9%	8.2%	10.7%
1999	82.0%	34.0%	15.8%	6.5%	9.3%
2000	82.7%	31.8%	12.5%	5.3%	7.2%
2001	81.1%	32.4%	10.6%	5.1%	5.5%
2002	80.3%	32.2%	10.0%	4.6%	5.4%
2003	78.7%	33.9%	12.0%	6.1%	5.9%
2004	77.7%	34.9%	10.1%	5.2%	4.9%
2005	77.6%	34.7%	10.5%	6.6%	3.9%
2006	77.3%	35.1%	9.1%	4.6%	4.4%
2007	77.9%	35.3%	8.2%	4.1%	4.1%
2008	76.9%	35.8%	9.0%	4.4%	4.6%
2009	74.0%	37.6%	8.8%	5.2%	3.6%

Source: Congressional Research Service (CRS) estimates based on analysis of U.S. Census Bureau 1988 to 2010 Current Population Survey (CPS) Annual Social and Economic Supplement (ASEC) data.

Notes: Details may not sum to totals due to rounding. Support table for Figure 8.

Table C-7. Employment Rates of Single and Married Mothers, by Age of Youngest Child, March 1988 to March 2010 (Percent of single mothers employed in March)

Year	Single Mothers				Married Mothers			
	With a Child Under Age 18	Youngest Child Under Age 3	Youngest Child Age 3 to 5	Youngest Child Age 6 to 17	With a Child Under Age 18	Youngest Child Under Age 3	Youngest Child Age 3 to 5	Youngest Child Age 6 to 17
1988	57.4%	35.1%	52.9%	69.1%	61.8%	50.7%	58.1%	69.6%
1989	58.2%	37.9%	53.1%	70.0%	63.0%	51.4%	60.8%	70.6%
1990	60.3%	38.0%	61.0%	70.9%	63.4%	52.7%	60.9%	70.8%
1991	58.1%	36.6%	55.7%	70.2%	63.1%	52.7%	60.5%	70.5%
1992	57.3%	35.2%	54.1%	69.8%	63.9%	53.1%	59.4%	71.9%
1993	57.3%	35.1%	54.8%	70.1%	63.9%	53.2%	59.4%	71.9%
1994	58.0%	37.7%	55.2%	69.3%	65.5%	56.0%	61.2%	72.6%
1995	61.1%	43.1%	58.5%	70.5%	67.1%	57.4%	63.9%	73.4%
1996	63.5%	44.7%	60.4%	72.9%	67.6%	58.2%	63.3%	74.2%
1997	65.6%	51.5%	64.3%	72.0%	68.5%	58.3%	64.4%	75.2%
1998	68.8%	54.8%	63.7%	76.4%	67.9%	58.3%	64.1%	74.2%
1999	70.7%	55.8%	69.8%	77.1%	67.9%	57.0%	63.1%	75.1%
2000	72.8%	59.1%	72.7%	78.5%	68.4%	56.8%	66.0%	75.0%
2001	72.5%	57.6%	71.3%	79.1%	68.0%	56.0%	64.2%	75.1%
2002	71.2%	57.9%	71.0%	76.3%	66.7%	54.9%	61.7%	74.1%
2003	69.6%	54.8%	69.3%	75.4%	66.3%	53.5%	61.7%	74.2%
2004	69.7%	54.1%	69.5%	75.7%	65.3%	52.4%	62.3%	72.7%
2005	68.9%	53.7%	66.7%	75.7%	65.9%	54.9%	61.9%	72.8%
2006	69.6%	57.0%	68.0%	75.1%	66.1%	55.4%	61.8%	73.1%
2007	70.0%	56.5%	68.6%	76.0%	67.3%	56.9%	63.0%	74.25
2008	69.1%	54.5%	68.5%	75.5%	67.0%	56.1%	63.6%	73.7%
2009	65.8%	52.5%	62.3%	72.9%	66.0%	56.3%	60.1%	72.7%
2010	64.1%	52.9%	59.7%	70.7%	65.3%	54.9%	62.6%	71.3%

Source: Congressional Research Service (CRS) estimates based on analysis of U.S. Census Bureau 1988 to 2010 Current Population Survey (CPS) Annual Social and Economic Supplement (ASEC) data.

Note: Support table for Figure 9.

Table C-8. Monthly Unemployment Rate of Women Who Maintain Families, January 1987 to June 2011 (Rates are not seasonally adjusted)

	Jan	Feb	Mar	Apr	May	Jun	Jul	Aug	Sep	Oct	Nov	Dec	Annual Average
1987	9.8	10.0	9.7	9.0	9.1	9.5	9.0	9.7	9.3	9.2	8.4	7.6	9.2
1988	8.9	8.6	7.5	8.2	8.1	7.9	8.2	7.9	8.5	8.1	7.5	7.6	8.1
1989	8.1	8.3	7.8	7.3	8.1	7.9	8.5	8.4	8.0	7.8	8.1	7.5	8.1
1990	7.8	7.9	8.3	7.2	7.4	8.1	8.8	9.0	9.4	8.8	8.7	8.4	8.3
1991	9.2	9.4	9.0	9.2	9.0	9.1	8.8	10.2	9.6	9.8	9.1	8.6	9.3
1992	9.2	9.8	9.9	9.8	9.7	10.2	11.0	11.4	9.6	9.4	10.4	9.7	10.0
1993	10.5	10.5	9.1	9.5	9.6	9.8	10.4	9.6	9.1	9.4	9.0	9.8	9.7
1994	9.5	9.9	9.5	8.9	8.6	8.7	8.3	9.4	8.7	8.8	8.1	8.7	8.9
1995	9.1	8.5	7.7	8.8	7.8	8.3	8.8	7.4	7.9	7.9	7.3	6.6	8.0
1996	8.4	7.7	7.4	7.0	8.3	7.6	9.7	9.0	8.3	8.5	8.4	8.1	8.2
1997	9.5	9.1	8.7	7.1	7.5	7.9	8.2	8.6	7.7	7.8	7.8	7.2	8.1
1998	8.3	7.9	7.6	6.8	7.2	6.8	7.3	7.2	7.5	6.9	6.9	5.8	7.2
1999	6.7	6.8	6.8	6.5	5.8	6.3	6.8	6.7	6.5	6.0	6.0	5.7	6.4
2000	6.6	6.4	7.0	5.8	6.3	5.9	5.9	6.4	5.4	5.3	5.1	4.5	5.9
2001	6.7	6.3	6.5	5.9	6.2	6.2	6.5	7.0	6.9	6.6	7.7	7.2	6.6
2002	8.2	8.3	7.9	8.2	8.1	8.2	8.6	7.6	7.0	7.7	8.0	7.9	8.0
2003	8.0	9.0	8.4	8.5	8.3	8.7	9.0	8.4	8.5	8.4	8.3	8.4	8.5
2004	8.3	8.1	8.4	7.5	7.4	8.2	9.0	8.3	8.2	7.8	7.7	7.1	8.0
2005	8.2	8.0	8.0	7.7	7.9	8.2	8.8	7.2	7.6	7.3	7.2	6.9	7.8

Table C-8. (Continued)

	Jan	Feb	Mar	Apr	May	Jun	Jul	Aug	Sep	Oct	Nov	Dec	Annual Average
2006	8.2	7.5	7.5	7.5	6.3	7.2	7.4	6.7	6.8	6.5	6.9	6.2	7.1
2007	6.6	6.5	6.7	6.2	6.3	6.8	6.8	6.2	6.4	6.3	6.6	6.9	6.5
2008	7.0	6.7	7.1	6.8	6.9	7.9	8.5	9.6	8.2	8.8	9.3	9.5	8.0
2009	10.3	10.3	10.8	10.0	11.0	11.7	12.6	12.2	11.6	12.9	11.4	13.0	11.5
2010	12.3	11.6	11.3	11.0	11.6	12.1	13.4	13.4	12.9	12.4	13.0	12.0	12.3
2011	12.7	13.0	12.3	11.7	12.7	12.8							

Source: U.S. Bureau of Labor Statistics. Data extracted from the internet on July 12, 2011. Data available at http://data.bls.gov/cgi-bin/srgate (Series: LNU04000313).

Note: Support table for Figure 10.

Table C-9. Poor Single Mothers: Work and Welfare Status During the Year, 1987 to 2009

Year	Number of Poor Single Mothers (in 000s)	Received Cash Welfare During Year	Received Cash Welfare but Did Not Work During Year	Combined Work and Welfare over the Year	Worked at Any Time During the Year	Worked but Did Not Receive Cash Welfare at Any Time During the Year	Neither Worked Nor Received Welfare During the Year
1987	3,661	61.8%	43.3%	18.5%	42.2%	23.7%	14.5%
1988	3,650	62.2%	43.0%	19.2%	43.5%	24.3%	13.5%
1989	3,506	58.6%	42.7%	15.9%	43.1%	27.2%	14.2%
1990	3,821	61.9%	41.4%	20.5%	46.0%	25.5%	12.6%
1991	4,101	62.1%	43.3%	18.8%	44.3%	25.5%	12.5%
1992	4,339	61.0%	42.1%	18.9%	43.6%	24.7%	14.3%
1993	4,456	61.4%	41.5%	19.8%	44.3%	24.5%	14.1%
1994	4,203	58.3%	37.8%	20.5%	47.3%	26.8%	14.9%
1995	3,971	54.2%	34.2%	20.0%	49.7%	29.7%	16.1%
1996	4,005	51.4%	31.1%	20.3%	52.6%	32.2%	16.4%
1997	3,946	44.0%	24.5%	19.5%	57.8%	38.3%	17.7%
1998	3,685	38.9%	19.2%	19.7%	60.4%	40.7%	20.4%
1999	3,314	33.1%	15.4%	17.8%	64.3%	46.5%	20.3%
2000	3,090	27.2%	13.6%	13.6%	61.6%	48.1%	24.8%
2001	3,259	23.2%	12.9%	10.4%	58.6%	48.2%	28.6%
2002	3,284	21.5%	11.8%	9.8%	59.0%	49.2%	29.3%
2003	3,525	26.0%	14.7%	11.2 %	56.5%	45.3%	28.7%
2004	3,648	20.8%	12.1%	8.7%	55.3%	46.6%	32.6%
2005	3,640	22.1%	13.2%	8.9%	54.0%	45.1%	32.8%
2006	3,841	18.8%	11.0%	7.8%	54.4%	46.7%	34.6%
2007	3,790	17.1%	10.0%	7.1%	55.9%	48.8%	34.1%
2008	3,863	18.2%	10.4%	7.8%	55.0%	47.2%	34.6%
2009	4,128	17.5%	11.4%	6.1%	51.6%	45.6%	37.0%

Source: Congressional Research Service (CRS) estimates based on analysis of U.S. Census Bureau 1988 to 2010 Current Population Survey (CPS) Annual Social and Economic Supplement (ASEC) data.

Note: Support table for Figure 11.

Table C-10. Receipt of Selected Benefits by Female-Headed Families with Children, All Families and "Earnings Poor" Families (Numbers in 1,000s)

Year	Total	Received AFDC, TANF, or GA		Received SSI		Received Food Stamps/SNAP		Received UI		Received Child Support		Received the EITC		Received the ACTC[a]	
		Num.	Pct.	Num.	Pct.	Num.	Pct.	Num.	Pct.	Num.	Pct.	Num.	Pct.	Num.	Pct.
All Families															
1987	8,193	2,719	33.2%	412	5.0%	2,958	36.1%	421	5.1%	2,322	28.3%	3,437	41.9%		
1988	8,321	2,737	32.9%	383	4.6%	3,034	36.5%	446	5.4%	2,286	27.5%	3,994	48.0%		
1989	8,400	2,537	30.2%	404	4.8%	2,860	34.0%	493	5.9%	2,451	29.2%	4,086	48.6%		
1990	8,745	2,901	33.2%	430	4.9%	3,260	37.3%	628	7.2%	2,531	28.9%	4,365	49.9%		
1991	9,031	3,101	34.3%	474	5.3%	3,572	39.6%	694	7.7%	2,603	28.8%	4,441	49.2%		
1992	9,567	3,300	34.5%	555	5.8%	3,981	41.6%	721	7.5%	2,849	29.8%	4,745	49.6%		
1993	9,860	3,439	34.9%	748	7.6%	4,295	43.6%	699	7.1%	2,968	30.1%	4,963	50.3%		
1994	9,837	3,166	32.2%	725	7.4%	4,036	41.0%	706	7.2%	3,097	31.5%	5,312	54.0%		
1995	9,887	2,862	28.9%	722	7.3%	3,755	38.0%	615	6.2%	3,263	33.0%	5,589	56.5%		
1996	10,052	2,669	26.6%	755	7.5%	3,674	36.5%	692	6.9%	3,204	31.9%	5,987	59.6%		
1997	9,874	2,225	22.5%	723	7.3%	3,291	33.3%	554	5.6%	3,015	30.5%	5,950	60.3%		
1998	9,881	1,872	18.9%	661	6.7%	3,019	30.6%	543	5.5%	3,077	31.1%	6,064	61.4%		
1999	9,741	1,543	15.8%	619	6.4%	2,491	25.6%	496	5.1%	3,158	32.4%	6,196	63.6%		
2000	9,712	1,215	12.5%	614	6.3%	2,298	23.7%	519	5.3%	3,194	32.9%	6,039	62.2%		
2001	10,044	1,064	10.6%	630	6.3%	2,433	24.2%	705	7.0%	3,387	33.7%	6,033	60.1%		
2002	10,206	1,025	10.0%	591	5.8%	2,574	25.2%	800	7.8%	3,330	32.6%	6,018	59.0%		
2003	10,411	1,253	12.0%	600	5.8%	2,758	26.5%	766	7.4%	3,333	32.0%	5,187	49.8%		
2004	10,442	1,054	10.1%	704	6.7%	2,918	27.9%	659	6.3%	3,373	32.3%	5,209	49.9%	3,876	37.1%
2005	10,476	1,102	10.5%	699	6.7%	3,005	28.7%	608	5.8%	3,205	30.6%	6,170	58.9%	3,384	32.3%
2006	10,938	991	9.1%	694	6.3%	2,982	27.3%	533	4.9%	3,233	29.6%	6,451	59.0%	3,625	33.1%

Year	Total	Received AFDC, TANF, or GA		Received SSI		Received Food Stamps/SNAP		Received UI		Received Child Support		Received the EITC		Received the ACTC[a]	
		Num.	Pct.	Num.	Pct.	Num.	Pct.	Num.	Pct.	Num.	Pct.	Num.	Pct.	Num.	Pct.
2007	10,748	878	8.2%	668	6.2%	2,979	27.7%	499	4.6%	3,157	29.4%	6,454	60.0%	3,526	32.8%
2008	10,797	974	9.0%	663	6.1%	3,464	32.1%	813	7.5%	3,044	28.2%	6,384	59.1%	3,366	31.2%
2009	10,990	967	8.8%	716	6.5%	3,908	35.6%	1,100	10.0%	3,004	27.3%	6,546	59.6%	4,976	45.3%
"Earnings Poor" Families															
1987	4,417	2,515	56.9%	352	8.0%	2,756	62.4%	206	4.7%	942	21.3%	1,798	40.7%		
1988	4,476	2,506	56.0%	312	7.0%	2,782	62.2%	198	4.4%	928	20.7%	1,940	43.3%		
1989	4,384	2,318	52.9%	318	7.3%	2,635	60.1%	224	5.1%	1,012	23.1%	1,959	44.7%		
1990	4,707	2,670	56.7%	353	7.5%	3,012	64.0%	261	5.5%	1,057	22.4%	2,159	45.9%		
1991	4,983	2,840	57.0%	412	8.3%	3,232	64.9%	320	6.4%	1,049	21.0%	2,277	45.7%		
1992	5,292	2,968	56.1%	469	8.9%	3,557	67.2%	398	7.5%	1,217	23.0%	2,372	44.8%		
1993	5,540	3,114	56.2%	611	11.0%	3,831	69.1%	362	6.5%	1,333	24.1%	2,425	43.8%		
1994	5,297	2,848	53.8%	623	11.8%	3,576	67.5%	344	6.5%	1,300	24.5%	2,609	49.3%		
1995	5,040	2,495	49.5%	585	11.6%	3,233	64.1%	307	6.1%	1,432	28.4%	2,635	52.3%		
1996	5,009	2,330	46.5%	633	12.6%	3,125	62.4%	333	6.7%	1,299	25.9%	2,722	54.3%		
1997	4,993	2,038	40.8%	574	11.5%	2,867	57.4%	300	6.0%	1,247	25.0%	2,821	56.5%		
1998	4,730	1,688	35.7%	548	11.6%	2,584	54.6%	289	6.1%	1,131	23.9%	2,895	61.2%		
1999	4,249	1,321	31.1%	474	11.2%	2,135	50.3%	230	5.4%	1,101	25.9%	2,720	64.0%		
2000	3,966	1,026	25.9%	462	11.7%	1,931	48.7%	200	5.0%	1,100	27.7%	2,508	63.2%		
2001	4,205	920	21.9%	484	11.5%	2,029	48.3%	307	7.3%	1,233	29.3%	2,502	59.5%		
2002	4,308	863	20.0%	451	10.5%	2,080	48.3%	414	9.6%	1,301	30.2%	2,531	58.8%		
2003	4,470	1,078	24.1%	465	10.4%	2,294	51.3%	380	8.5%	1,293	28.9%	2,182	48.8%		
2004	4,625	913	19.7%	526	11.4%	2,428	52.5%	317	6.9%	1,326	28.7%	2,219	48.0%	1,187	25.7%
2005	4,605	956	20.8%	571	12.4%	2,487	54.0%	285	6.2%	1,225	26.6%	2,636	57.2%	874	19.0%
2006	4,866	844	17.3%	548	11.3%	2,554	52.5%	256	5.3%	1,346	27.7%	2,800	57.5%	1,008	20.7%

Table C-10. (Continued)

Year	Total	Received AFDC, TANF, or GA		Received SSI		Received Food Stamps/SNAP		Received UI		Received Child Support		Received the EITC		Received the ACTC[a]	
		Num.	Pct.	Num.	Pct.	Num.	Pct.	Num.	Pct.	Num.	Pct.	Num.	Pct.	Num.	Pct.
2007	4,801	765	15.9%	533	11.1%	2,456	51.2%	223	4.7%	1,303	27.1%	2,846	59.3%	1,085	22.6%
2008	4,961	838	16.9%	524	10.6%	2,787	56.2%	381	7.7%	1,258	25.4%	2,954	59.5%	1,067	21.5%
2009	5,313	864	16.3%	575	10.8%	3,197	60.2%	607	11.4%	1,345	25.3%	3,072	57.8%	2,433	45.8%

Source: Congressional Research Service (CRS) estimates based on analysis of U.S. Census Bureau 1988 to 2010 Current Population Survey (CPS) Annual Social and Economic Supplement (ASEC) data.

Notes: "Earnings poor" families whose annual earned income is below their poverty income threshold. Other sources of income received by these families might subsequently lift their total income above poverty.

Support table for Figure 12.

a. The Economic Growth and Tax Relief Reconciliation Act of 2001 (EGTRRA; P.L. 107-16) made the Child Tax Credit (CTC) partially refundable. Beginning in 2004, the Census Bureau began modeling the Additional Child Tax Credit (ACTC), the refundable portion of the CTC, on the CPS/ASEC.

Table C-11. Effect of Earnings, Transfers, and Taxes on Family Poverty and Household Low-Income Status, All Single Mothers, 1987 to 2009 (Numbers in 1,000s)

Year	Number of Families	Poverty Rates by Income Concept										
		Earned Income Only	+ Cash, Other Than Child Support,UI, and CashWelfare	+ Child Support	+ UI Benefits	+ SSI	+ AFDC, TANF, GA ("Official Poverty Rate")	+ Food Stamp/ SNAP Benefits	+ EITC Less FICA and Federal and State Income Taxes	+ ACTC	+ Economic Stimulus and Recovery Payments	Total House-hold After-Tax Income
1987	8,193	53.9%	49.2%	47.4%	47.1%	46.6%	44.7%	42.3%	42.6%	42.6%	42.6%	39.5%
1988	8,321	53.8%	48.6%	46.5%	46.1%	45.9%	43.9%	42.2%	42.1%	42.1%	42.1%	38.9%
1989	8,400	52.2%	46.8%	44.4%	44.0%	43.7%	41.7%	39.7%	39.9%	39.9%	39.9%	36.3%
1990	8,745	53.8%	49.0%	46.9%	46.6%	46.1%	43.7%	41.5%	41.2%	41.2%	41.2%	37.4%
1991	9,031	55.2%	50.1%	48.3%	47.8%	47.4%	45.4%	42.8%	42.2%	42.2%	42.2%	38.0%
1992	9,567	55.3%	50.8%	48.8%	48.2%	47.4%	45.4%	42.5%	41.7%	41.7%	41.7%	37.5%
1993	9,860	56.2%	50.9%	48.7%	48.1%	47.4%	45.2%	42.7%	41.9%	41.9%	41.9%	37.8%
1994	9,837	53.9%	48.5%	46.5%	46.0%	45.5%	42.7%	39.8%	37.5%	37.5%	37.5%	33.3%
1995	9,887	51.0%	46.4%	43.6%	43.2%	42.3%	40.2%	36.9%	33.4%	33.4%	33.4%	30.0%
1996	10,052	49.8%	45.2%	43.1%	42.6%	41.5%	39.8%	37.1%	33.9%	33.9%	33.9%	30.2%
1997	9,874	50.6%	45.1%	43.0%	42.6%	41.7%	40.0%	37.7%	33.5%	33.5%	33.5%	29.2%
1998	9,881	47.9%	42.6%	40.1%	39.5%	38.8%	37.3%	35.2%	30.8%	30.8%	30.8%	27.3%

Table C-11. (Continued)

Year	Number of Families	Poverty Rates by Income Concept										
		Earned Income Only	+ Cash, Other Than Child Support,UI, and CashWelfare	+ Child Support	+ UI Benefits	+ SSI	+ AFDC, TANF, GA ("Official Poverty Rate")	+ Food Stamp/ SNAP Benefits	+ EITC Less FICA and Federal and State Income Taxes	+ ACTC	+ Economic Stimulus and Recovery Payments	Total House-hold After-Tax Income
1999	9,741	43.6%	38.9%	36.7%	36.3%	35.3%	34.0%	32.2%	28.5%	28.5%	28.5%	24.7%
2000	9,712	40.8%	36.0%	33.9%	33.7%	32.8%	31.8%	30.5%	26.8%	26.8%	26.8%	22.8%
2001	10,044	41.9%	37.6%	34.9%	34.3%	33.3%	32.4%	30.9%	27.2%	27.2%	27.2%	23.4%
2002	10,206	42.2%	37.1%	34.8%	33.8%	32.9%	32.2%	30.5%	26.6%	26.6%	26.6%	23.4%
2003	10,411	42.9%	38.4%	36.1%	35.3%	34.5%	33.9%	32.2%	29.0%	29.0%	29.0%	24.8%
2004	10,442	44.3%	39.6%	37.1%	36.5%	35.7%	34.9%	32.5%	29.9%	29.2%	29.2%	24.8%
2005	10,476	44.0%	39.5%	37.0%	36.4%	35.5%	34.7%	32.6%	28.9%	28.5%	28.5%	24.4%
2006	10,938	44.5%	39.6%	37.5%	36.9%	35.7%	35.1%	32.9%	29.2%	28.7%	28.7%	23.7%
2007	10,748	44.7%	39.4%	37.1%	36.7%	35.8%	35.3%	33.1%	29.1%	28.8%	28.8%	24.4%
2008	10,797	45.9%	40.5%	38.1%	37.3%	36.3%	35.8%	33.3%	29.7%	29.4%	28.3%	23.8%
2009	10,990	48.3%	42.6%	40.3%	38.9%	38.0%	37.6%	33.5%	29.6%	27.9%	27.3%	22.6%

Source: Congressional Research Service (CRS) estimates based on analysis of U.S. Census Bureau 1988 to 2010 Current Population Survey (CPS) Annual Social and Economic Supplement (ASEC) data.

Note: Support table for Figure 13.

Table C-12. Effect of Earnings, Transfers, and Taxes on Family Poverty and Household Low-Income Status, Single Mothers Who Worked at Any Time During the Year, 1987 to 2009 (Numbers in 1,000s)

Year	Number of Families	Poverty Rates by Income Concept										
		Earned Income Only	+ Cash, Other than Child Support, UI, and Cash Welfare	+ Child Support	+ UI Benefits	+ SSI	+ AFDC, TANF, GA ("Official Poverty Rate")	+ Food Stamp/SNAP Benefits	+ EITC Less FICA and Federal and State Income Taxes	+ ACTC	+ Economic Stimulus and Recovery Payments	Total House-hold After-TaxIncome
1987	5,518	36.8%	32.3%	30.1%	29.7%	29.4%	28.0%	26.1%	26.1%	26.1%	26.1%	23.4%
1988	5,733	37.5%	32.6%	29.9%	29.4%	29.2%	27.7%	26.5%	26.3%	26.3%	26.3%	23.8%
1989	5,891	35.9%	30.9%	27.9%	27.4%	27.2%	25.7%	23.8%	23.9%	23.9%	23.9%	21.0%
1990	6,108	38.5%	33.7%	31.3%	30.8%	30.4%	28.8%	27.1%	26.4%	26.4%	26.4%	23.5%
1991	6,205	38.8%	33.8%	31.7%	31.0%	30.6%	29.3%	26.9%	26.0%	26.0%	26.0%	22.5%
1992	6,433	38.9%	34.6%	32.2%	31.4%	30.9%	29.4%	27.0%	25.9%	25.9%	25.9%	22.4%
1993	6,717	39.7%	35.0%	32.3%	31.5%	31.0%	29.4%	27.5%	26.1%	26.1%	26.1%	22.6%
1994	7,022	38.8%	33.9%	31.5%	30.9%	30.6%	28.3%	26.0%	22.7%	22.7%	22.7%	19.3%
1995	7,220	37.4%	33.4%	30.0%	29.5%	28.9%	27.3%	24.6%	19.9%	19.9%	19.9%	17.3%
1996	7,548	37.1%	32.6%	30.1%	29.4%	28.8%	27.9%	25.5%	21.1%	21.1%	21.1%	17.9%
1997	7,636	39.0%	34.5%	32.1%	31.6%	31.1%	29.9%	27.8%	22.3%	22.3%	22.3%	18.6%
1998	7,868	38.0%	33.5%	30.7%	30.0%	29.7%	28.3%	26.3%	20.9%	20.9%	20.9%	18.2%

Table C-12. (Continued)

Year	Number of Families	Poverty Rates by Income Concept										
		Earned Income Only	+ Cash, Other than Child Support, UI, and Cash Welfare	+ Child Support	+ UI Benefits	+ SSI	+ AFDC, TANF, GA ("Official Poverty Rate")	+ Food Stamp/SNAP Benefits	+ EITC Less FICA and Federal and State Income Taxes	+ ACTC	+ Economic Stimulus and Recovery Payments	Total House-hold After-TaxIncome
1999	7,986	34.7%	30.9%	28.7%	28.2%	27.6%	26.7%	25.1%	20.6%	20.6%	20.6%	17.7%
2000	8,030	31.6%	27.4%	25.2%	24.9%	24.4%	23.7%	22.6%	18.1%	18.1%	18.1%	15.0%
2001	8,148	31.5%	28.3%	25.3%	24.6%	24.0%	23.4%	22.0%	17.6%	17.6%	17.6%	14.8%
2002	8,193	31.9%	28.0%	25.7%	24.6%	24.1%	23.6%	22.2%	17.3%	17.3%	17.3%	14.8%
2003	8,191	32.0%	28.7%	26.1%	25.2%	24.7%	24.3%	22.8%	18.7%	18.7%	18.7%	15.8%
2004	8,110	32.5%	28.8%	26.4%	25.7%	25.3%	24.9%	22.7%	19.1%	18.4%	18.4%	15.2%
2005	8,124	32.0%	28.5%	25.9%	25.2%	24.7%	24.2%	22.1%	17.1%	16.7%	16.7%	13.7%
2006	8,458	32.6%	28.6%	26.5%	25.9%	25.1%	24.7%	22.6%	17.5%	17.0%	17.0%	13.2%
2007	8,372	33.2%	29.2%	26.6%	26.3%	25.7%	25.3%	23.1%	17.6%	17.3%	17.3%	14.2%
2008	8,301	34.2%	30.1%	27.6%	26.8%	25.9%	25.6%	23.2%	18.3%	18.0%	16.7%	13.7%
2009	8,133	35.6%	30.7%	28.3%	27.1%	26.5%	26.2%	22.5%	17.0%	14.9%	14.2%	11.2%

Source: Congressional Research Service (CRS) estimates based on analysis of U.S. Census Bureau 1988 to 2010 Current Population Survey (CPS) Annual Social and Economic Supplement (ASEC) data.

Note: Support table for Figure 14.

Table C-13. Effect of Earnings, Transfers, and Taxes on Family Poverty and Household Low-Income Status, Single Mothers Who Did Not Work at Any Time During the Year, 1987 to 2009 (Numbers in 1,000s)

Year	Number of Families	Poverty Rates by Income Concept										
		Earned Income Only	+ Cash, Other than Child Support, UI, and Cash Welfare	+ Child Support	+ UI Benefits	+ SSI	+ AFDC, TANF, GA ("Official Poverty Rate")	+ Food Stamp/SNAP Benefits	+ EITC Less FICA and Federal and State Income Taxes	+ ACTC	+ Economic Stimulus and Recovery Payments	Total House-hold After-axIncome
1987	2,676	89.1%	84.2%	83.3%	83.0%	82.1%	79.1%	75.7%	76.5%	76.5%	76.5%	72.9%
1988	2,588	89.8%	84.2%	83.4%	83.3%	82.8%	79.7%	76.8%	77.2%	77.2%	77.2%	72.3%
1989	2,510	90.3%	84.0%	83.0%	83.0%	82.5%	79.5%	76.8%	77.3%	77.3%	77.3%	72.3%
1990	2,637	89.3%	84.2%	83.2%	83.1%	82.3%	78.3%	74.9%	75.4%	75.4%	75.4%	69.5%
1991	2,826	91.2%	85.8%	84.8%	84.6%	84.1%	80.8%	77.6%	77.9%	77.9%	77.9%	72.0%
1992	3,135	89.0%	83.9%	83.0%	82.7%	81.2%	78.1%	74.2%	74.3%	74.3%	74.3%	68.5%
1993	3,144	91.5%	84.9%	83.8%	83.5%	82.6%	78.9%	75.1%	75.6%	75.6%	75.6%	70.3%
1994	2,815	91.5%	84.9%	83.9%	83.7%	82.7%	78.7%	74.2%	74.5%	74.5%	74.5%	68.1%
1995	2,667	87.6%	81.7%	80.5%	80.4%	78.6%	74.9%	70.2%	69.9%	69.9%	69.9%	64.2%
1996	2,504	88.2%	83.3%	82.4%	82.1%	79.5%	75.9%	72.2%	72.5%	72.5%	72.5%	66.9%
1997	2,238	90.1%	81.3%	80.2%	80.1%	77.8%	74.4%	71.5%	71.6%	71.6%	71.6%	65.2%
1998	2,013	86.3%	77.8%	76.6%	76.5%	74.3%	72.5%	69.8%	69.2%	69.2%	69.2%	62.8%

Table C-13. (Continued)

Year	Number of Families	Poverty Rates by Income Concept										
		Earned Income Only	+ Cash, Other than Child Support, UI, and Cash Welfare	+ Child Support	+ UI Benefits	+ SSI	+ AFDC, TANF, GA ("Official Poverty Rate")	+ Food Stamp/SNAP Benefits	+ EITC Less FICA and Federal and State Income Taxes	+ ACTC	+ Economic Stimulus and Recovery Payments	Total House-hold After-axIncome
1999	1,755	84.4%	75.3%	73.6%	73.3%	70.8%	67.4%	65.0%	64.9%	64.9%	64.9%	56.5%
2000	1,682	84.8%	77.0%	75.8%	75.5%	72.9%	70.5%	68.3%	68.6%	68.6%	68.6%	60.0%
2001	1,896	86.5%	77.5%	76.1%	75.6%	73.3%	71.2%	69.1%	68.9%	68.9%	68.9%	60.3%
2002	2,013	84.0%	74.0%	72.0%	71.2%	68.7%	66.9%	64.6%	64.9%	64.9%	64.9%	58.5%
2003	2,220	83.1%	74.0%	72.8%	72.5%	70.5%	69.0%	66.8%	66.7%	66.7%	66.7%	58.0%
2004	2,332	85.2%	76.8%	74.4%	73.9%	71.7%	69.9%	66.6%	67.2%	66.7%	66.7%	58.2%
2005	2,352	85.4%	77.8%	75.7%	75.3%	72.7%	71.2%	68.9%	69.7%	69.4%	69.4%	61.3%
2006	2,479	85.0%	76.8%	75.1%	74.4%	72.0%	70.6%	67.9%	68.9%	68.8%	68.8%	59.7%
2007	2,376	85.1%	75.5%	73.9%	73.4%	71.3%	70.3%	68.5%	69.6%	69.5%	69.5%	60.3%
2008	2,496	85.1%	75.0%	72.9%	72.3%	70.6%	69.6%	67.0%	67.5%	67.5%	66.9%	57.3%
2009	2,856	84.7%	76.5%	74.6%	72.6%	70.8%	69.9%	64.7%	65.2%	64.8%	64.5%	55.1%

Source: Congressional Research Service (CRS) estimates based on analysis of U.S. Census Bureau 1988 to 2010 Current Population Survey (CPS) Annual Social and Economic Supplement (ASEC) data.

Note: Support table for Figure 15.

Table C-14. Single Mothers' Living Arrangements, by Mothers' Work and Welfare Status, 1987 to 2009 (Numbers in 1,000s)

Year	Total		Independent Families		Lives with Others							
					Total		Extended Families		Cohabiting[a]		Unrelated Families[a]	
	Number	Percent	Number	Percent	Number	Percent	Number	Percent	Number	Percent	Number	Percent
1987	8,193	100.0%	5,526	67.4%	2,668	32.6%	1,703	20.8%	590	7.2%	375	4.6%
1988	8,321	100.0%	5,703	68.5%	2,618	31.5%	1,667	20.0%	603	7.3%	348	4.2%
1989	8,400	100.0%	5,681	67.6%	2,720	32.4%	1,650	19.6%	603	7.2%	466	5.6%
1990	8,745	100.0%	5,916	67.7%	2,829	32.3%	1,693	19.4%	695	7.9%	441	5.0%
1991	9,031	100.0%	5,993	66.4%	3,038	33.6%	1,690	18.7%	835	9.2%	512	5.7%
1992	9,567	100.0%	6,294	65.8%	3,273	34.2%	1,872	19.6%	880	9.2%	522	5.5%
1993	9,860	100.0%	6,555	66.5%	3,306	33.5%	1,890	19.2%	849	8.6%	567	5.7%
1994	9,837	100.0%	6,357	64.6%	3,479	35.4%	1,968	20.0%	914	9.3%	597	6.1%
1995	9,887	100.0%	6,347	64.2%	3,536	35.8%	2,030	20.5%	948	9.6%	562	5.7%
1996	10,052	100.0%	6,593	65.6%	3,456	34.4%	1,930	19.2%	945	9.4%	584	5.8%
1997	9,874	100.0%	6,362	64.4%	3,511	35.6%	1,966	19.9%	967	9.8%	580	5.9%
1998	9,881	100.0%	6,497	65.8%	3,382	34.2%	1,884	19.1%	951	9.6%	549	5.6%
1999	9,741	100.0%	6,217	63.8%	3,524	36.2%	1,882	19.3%	1,064	10.9%	578	5.9%
2000	9,712	100.0%	6,160	63.4%	3,552	36.6%	1,913	19.7%	1,076	11.1%	563	5.8%

Table C-14. (Continued)

Year	Total		Independent Families		Lives with Others							
					Total		Extended Families		Cohabiting[a]		Unrelated Families[a]	
	Number	Percent	Number	Percent	Number	Percent	Number	Percent	Number	Percent	Number	Percent
2001	10,044	100.0%	6,639	66.1%	3,405	33.9%	1,831	18.2%	999	9.9%	574	5.7%
2002	10,206	100.0%	6,714	65.8%	3,492	34.2%	1,825	17.9%	1,050	10.3%	617	6.0%
2003	10,411	100.0%	6,745	64.8%	3,664	35.2%	1,950	18.7%	1,062	10.2%	654	6.3%
2004	10,442	100.0%	6,820	65.3%	3,622	34.7%	1,946	18.6%	1,031	9.9%	646	6.2%
2005	10,476	100.0%	6,866	65.5%	3,610	34.5%	1,882	18.0%	1,103	10.5%	624	6.0%
2006	10,938	100.0%	6,905	63.1%	4,033	36.9%	2,136	19.5%	1,581[a]	14.5%[a]	315[a]	2.9%[a]
2007	10,748	100.0%	6,791	63.2%	3,957	36.8%	2,101	19.5%	1,581[a]	14.7%[a]	275[a]	2.6%[a]
2008	10,797	100.0%	6,814	63.1%	3,983	36.9%	2,177	20.2%	1,503[a]	13.9%[a]	303[a]	2.8%[a]
2009	10,990	100.0%	6,592	60.0%	4,398	40.0%	2,345	21.3%	1,647[a]	15.0%[a]	406[a]	3.7%[a]
Worked During the Year												
1987	5,434	100.0%	3,743	68.9%	1,691	31.1%	984	18.1%	417	7.7%	291	5.3%
1988	5,646	100.0%	3,989	70.7%	1,656	29.3%	961	17.0%	444	7.9%	251	4.5%
1989	5,832	100.0%	4,011	68.8%	1,821	31.2%	1,021	17.5%	433	7.4%	368	6.3%
1990	5,998	100.0%	4,179	69.7%	1,820	30.3%	1,005	16.8%	489	8.2%	325	5.4%
1991	6,134	100.0%	4,146	67.6%	1,988	32.4%	982	16.0%	604	9.8%	402	6.6%

Year	Total		Independent Families		Lives with Others							
					Total		Extended Families		Cohabiting[a]		Unrelated Families[a]	
	Number	Percent	Number	Percent	Number	Percent	Number	Percent	Number	Percent	Number	Percent
1992	6,326	100.0%	4,330	68.4%	1,996	31.6%	1,019	16.1%	612	9.7%	365	5.8%
1993	6,580	100.0%	4,432	67.4%	2,147	32.6%	1,130	17.2%	601	9.1%	417	6.3%
1994	6,920	100.0%	4,544	65.7%	2,375	34.3%	1,229	17.8%	678	9.8%	468	6.8%
1995	7,108	100.0%	4,703	66.2%	2,401	33.8%	1,254	17.6%	705	9.9%	446	6.3%
1996	7,435	100.0%	4,960	66.7%	2,474	33.3%	1,288	17.3%	753	10.1%	434	5.8%
1997	7,578	100.0%	4,989	65.8%	2,588	34.2%	1,360	18.0%	763	10.1%	465	6.1%
1998	7,759	100.0%	5,259	67.8%	2,501	32.2%	1,273	16.4%	771	9.9%	457	5.9%
1999	7,913	100.0%	5,268	66.6%	2,646	33.4%	1,288	16.3%	884	11.2%	474	6.0%
2000	7,971	100.0%	5,187	65.1%	2,784	34.9%	1,417	17.8%	899	11.3%	468	5.9%
2001	8,058	100.0%	5,467	67.8%	2,591	32.2%	1,303	16.2%	793	9.8%	495	6.1%
2002	8,107	100.0%	5,458	67.3%	2,649	32.7%	1,268	15.6%	861	10.6%	521	6.4%
2003	8,111	100.0%	5,476	67.5%	2,633	32.5%	1,315	16.2%	804	9.9%	516	6.4%
2004	8,051	100.0%	5,451	67.7%	2,599	32.3%	1,273	15.8%	818	10.2%	508	6.3%
2005	8,048	100.0%	5,439	67.6%	2,609	32.4%	1,264	15.7%	843	10.5%	502	6.2%
2006	8,381	100.0%	5,512	65.8%	2,869	34.2%	1,421	17.0%	1,212[a]	14.5%[a]	235[a]	2.8%[a]

Table C-14. (Continued)

Year	Total		Independent Families		Lives with Others							
					Total		Extended Families		Cohabiting[a]		Unrelated Families[a]	
	Number	Percent	Number	Percent	Number	Percent	Number	Percent	Number	Percent	Number	Percent
2007	8,292	100.0%	5,509	66.4%	2,784	33.6%	1,389	16.7%	1,180[a]	14.2%[a]	215[a]	2.6%[a]
2008	8,223	100.0%	5,454	66.3%	2,768	33.7%	1,425	17.3%	1,110[a]	13.5%[a]	233[a]	2.8%[a]
2009	8,033	100.0%	5,066	63.1%	2,966	36.9%	1,495	18.6%	1,169[a]	14.6%[a]	303[a]	3.8%[a]
Did Not Work During Year												
1987	2,759	100.0%	1,783	64.6%	976	35.4%	719	26.1%	173	6.3%	84	3.0%
1988	2,675	100.0%	1,714	64.1%	962	35.9%	705	26.4%	160	6.0%	97	3.6%
1989	2,569	100.0%	1,670	65.0%	899	35.0%	629	24.5%	171	6.6%	99	3.8%
1990	2,746	100.0%	1,737	63.3%	1,009	36.7%	688	25.0%	206	7.5%	115	4.2%
1991	2,897	100.0%	1,847	63.8%	1,049	36.2%	709	24.5%	231	8.0%	110	3.8%
1992	3,241	100.0%	1,964	60.6%	1,277	39.4%	852	26.3%	268	8.3%	156	4.8%
1993	3,281	100.0%	2,122	64.7%	1,158	35.3%	760	23.2%	248	7.6%	150	4.6%
1994	2,917	100.0%	1,813	62.2%	1,104	37.8%	739	25.3%	236	8.1%	129	4.4%
1995	2,779	100.0%	1,644	59.2%	1,135	40.8%	776	27.9%	243	8.7%	116	4.2%
1996	2,616	100.0%	1,633	62.4%	981	37.5%	642	24.5%	192	7.3%	149	5.7%
1997	2,297	100.0%	1,372	59.7%	923	40.2%	605	26.4%	204	8.9%	116	5.0%

Year	Total		Independent Families		Lives with Others							
					Total		Extended Families		Cohabiting[a]		Unrelated Families[a]	
	Number	Percent	Number	Percent	Number	Percent	Number	Percent	Number	Percent	Number	Percent
1998	2,122	100.0%	1,238	58.4%	881	41.5%	611	28.8%	181	8.5%	92	4.3%
1999	1,827	100.0%	950	52.0%	878	48.0%	594	32.5%	180	9.8%	104	5.7%
2000	1,742	100.0%	973	55.9%	768	44.1%	497	28.5%	177	10.2%	95	5.4%
2001	1,986	100.0%	1,172	59.0%	813	41.0%	528	26.6%	206	10.4%	79	4.0%
2002	2,099	100.0%	1,256	59.8%	843	40.2%	557	26.5%	190	9.0%	96	4.6%
2003	2,300	100.0%	1,268	55.2%	1,031	44.8%	636	27.7%	258	11.2%	137	6.0%
2004	2,392	100.0%	1,369	57.2%	1,023	42.8%	672	28.1%	213	8.9%	138	5.8%
2005	2,428	100.0%	1,427	58.8%	1,001	41.2%	618	25.5%	261	10.7%	121	5.0%
2006	2,556	100.0%	1,392	54.5%	1,164	45.5%	715	28.0%	369[a]	14.4%[a]	80[a]	3.1%[a]
2007	2,456	100.0%	1,283	52.2%	1,173	47.8%	712	29.0%	401[a]	16.3%[a]	60[a]	2.5%[a]
2008	2,574	100.0%	1,359	52.8%	1,215	47.2%	752	29.2%	393[a]	15.3%[a]	70[a]	2.7%[a]
2009	2,957	100.0%	1,525	51.6%	1,431	48.4%	851	28.8%	478[a]	16.2%[a]	103[a]	3.5%[a]
Received Welfare During the Year												
1987	2,905	100.0%	1,995	68.7%	910	31.3%	654	22.5%	156	5.4%	99	3.4%
1988	2,919	100.0%	2,074	71.0%	845	29.0%	614	21.0%	174	6.0%	57	2.0%

Table C-14. (Continued)

Year	Total		Independent Families		Lives with Others							
					Total		Extended Families		Cohabiting[a]		Unrelated Families[a]	
	Number	Percent	Number	Percent	Number	Percent	Number	Percent	Number	Percent	Number	Percent
1989	2,717	100.0%	1,908	70.2%	809	29.8%	552	20.3%	154	5.7%	103	3.8%
1990	3,081	100.0%	2,137	69.4%	944	30.6%	655	21.3%	196	6.4%	92	3.0%
1991	3,296	100.0%	2,225	67.5%	1,071	32.5%	696	21.1%	241	7.3%	135	4.1%
1992	3,545	100.0%	2,399	67.7%	1,146	32.3%	769	21.7%	234	6.6%	142	4.0%
1993	3,757	100.0%	2,561	68.2%	1,197	31.8%	742	19.7%	269	7.2%	185	4.9%
1994	3,470	100.0%	2,330	67.2%	1,140	32.8%	702	20.2%	306	8.8%	132	3.8%
1995	3,247	100.0%	2,102	64.7%	1,145	35.3%	770	23.7%	260	8.0%	114	3.5%
1996	3,075	100.0%	2,079	67.6%	994	32.3%	640	20.8%	212	6.9%	144	4.7%
1997	2,646	100.0%	1,764	66.7%	882	33.3%	573	21.7%	195	7.4%	114	4.3%
1998	2,265	100.0%	1,636	72.2%	629	27.8%	386	17.0%	159	7.0%	85	3.7%
1999	1,950	100.0%	1,258	64.5%	692	35.5%	452	23.2%	150	7.7%	90	4.6%
2000	1,647	100.0%	1,122	68.2%	524	31.8%	357	21.7%	124	7.5%	44	2.7%
2001	1,524	100.0%	1,031	67.6%	493	32.4%	335	22.0%	102	6.7%	57	3.7%
2002	1,464	100.0%	1,017	69.5%	447	30.5%	298	20.4%	102	6.9%	47	3.2%
2003	1,673	100.0%	1,143	68.3%	530	31.7%	348	20.8%	136	8.1%	46	2.8%

Year	Total		Independent Families		Lives with Others							
					Total		Extended Families		Cohabiting[a]		Unrelated Families[a]	
	Number	Percent	Number	Percent	Number	Percent	Number	Percent	Number	Percent	Number	Percent
2004	1,592	100.0%	1,087	68.3%	505	31.7%	353	22.2%	87	5.5%	65	4.1%
2005	1,617	100.0%	1,153	71.3%	464	28.7%	284	17.6%	116	7.1%	64	4.0%
2006	1,526	100.0%	1,068	70.0%	458	30.0%	256	16.8%	176[a]	11.5%[a]	27[a]	1.7%[a]
2007	1,419	100.0%	972	68.5%	447	31.5%	316	22.2%	105[a]	7.4%[a]	27[a]	1.9%[a]
2008	1,507	100.0%	1,031	68.4%	476	31.6%	298	19.8%	145[a]	9.6%[a]	33[a]	2.2%[a]
2009	1,527	100.0%	950	62.2%	577	37.8%	363	23.8%	169[a]	11.1%[a]	45[a]	3.0%[a]

Source: Congressional Research Service (CRS) estimates based on analysis of U.S. Census Bureau 1988 to 2010 Current Population Survey (CPS) Annual Social and Economic Supplement (ASEC) data.

Notes: Independent families are families headed by a single mother with no other members other than her children. Extended families include mothers and their children who live with other family members. Cohabiting mothers live with another unrelated member who is identified or inferred to be a co-resident partner. Mothers in unrelated families co-reside with other unrelated household members, other than those identified or inferred to be a cohabiting partner.

Support table for Figure 16.

a. Beginning with the 2007 CPS/ASEC, cohabiting couples are identifiable based on self-report. In earlier years, cohabiting couples are identifiable indirectly by inference. The method used here, for CPS/ASEC years before 2007, is based on households with two unmarried adults, who are unrelated and of the opposite sex, and no other adults reside in the household. As a result, estimates for single mothers who are cohabiting or in unrelated families in CPS/ASEC years 2007 and after are not comparable to earlier years.

Table C-15. Poverty Status of Children in Female-Headed Families Under Selected Income Measures, 1987 to 2009 (Numbers in 1,000s)

Year	Total	Poor Based on Earned Income Only		Poor Based on Total Cash Income "Official" Poverty Measure		Poor Based on Cash Income Plus Food Stamp/SNAP Benefits, EITC and ACTC Net of Federal and State Income Taxes, Plus Stimulus and Recovery Payments		Below Household Low-Income Threshold Based on Total Household Income	
		Number	Percent	Number	Percent	Number	Percent	Number	Percent
1987	13,617	8,360	61.4%	7,081	52.0%	6,822	50.1%	6,437	47.3%
1988	13,700	8,406	61.4%	7,088	51.7%	6,827	49.8%	6,453	47.1%
1989	13,874	8,310	59.9%	6,904	49.8%	6,582	47.4%	6,083	43.8%
1990	14,608	9,003	61.6%	7,615	52.1%	7,258	49.7%	6,712	45.9%
1991	15,396	9,682	62.9%	8,223	53.4%	7,712	50.1%	7,092	46.1%
1992	15,586	9,724	62.4%	8,252	52.9%	7,660	49.1%	7,042	45.2%
1993	16,338	10,311	63.1%	8,532	52.2%	8,026	49.1%	7,346	45.0%
1994	16,480	10,132	61.5%	8,367	50.8%	7,444	45.2%	6,791	41.2%
1995	16,993	10,038	59.1%	8,221	48.4%	7,002	41.2%	6,457	38.0%
1996	16,740	9,547	57.0%	7,861	47.0%	6,780	40.5%	6,108	36.5%
1997	16,639	9,615	57.8%	7,907	47.5%	6,713	40.3%	6,023	36.2%
1998	16,833	9,280	55.1%	7,541	44.8%	6,311	37.5%	5,752	34.2%
1999	16,172	8,171	50.5%	6,515	40.3%	5,468	33.8%	4,844	30.0%
2000	16,120	7,733	48.0%	6,216	38.6%	5,294	32.8%	4,640	28.8%

Year	Total	Poor Based on Earned Income Only		Poor Based on Total Cash Income "Official" Poverty Measure		Poor Based on Cash Income Plus Food Stamp/SNAP Benefits, EITC and ACTC Net of Federal and State Income Taxes, Plus Stimulus and Recovery Payments		Below Household Low-Income Threshold Based on Total Household Income	
		Number	Percent	Number	Percent	Number	Percent	Number	Percent
2001	16,483	7,981	48.4%	6,334	38.4%	5,407	32.8%	4,755	28.8%
2002	16,780	8,202	48.9%	6,443	38.4%	5,341	31.8%	4,810	28.7%
2003	17,116	8,492	49.6%	6,868	40.1%	5,895	34.4%	5,211	30.4%
2004	17,229	8,725	50.6%	7,065	41.0%	5,805	33.7%	5,100	29.6%
2005	17,162	8,654	50.4%	7,077	41.2%	5,820	33.9%	5,084	29.6%
2006	17,921	9,111	50.8%	7,371	41.1%	6,025	33.6%	5,272	29.4%
2007	18,178	9,195	50.6%	7,511	41.3%	6,056	33.3%	5,268	29.0%
2008	18,086	9,390	51.9%	7,536	41.7%	6,502	36.0%	5,626	31.1%
2009	18,706	10,114	54.1%	8,113	43.4%	6,011	32.1%	5,222	27.9%

Source: Congressional Research Service (CRS) estimates based on analysis of U.S. Census Bureau 1988 to 2010 Current Population Survey (CPS) Annual Social and Economic Supplement (ASEC) data.

Note: Support table for Figure 19.

Table C-16. Single Mothers' Work Status During the Year and Self-Reported Reason for Not Working, by Cash Welfare (AFDC/TANF/GA SSI) Receipt, 1987 to 2009 (Numbers in 1,000s)

Year	Total	Worked		Did Not Work During the Year—Primary Reason for Not Working												
				Total			Ill or Disabled		Taking Care of Home or Family		Attending School		Could Not Find Work		Retired or Other	
		Num.	Pct.	Num.	Pct.	Sub-total Pct.	Num.	Pct.	Num.	Pct.	Num.	Pct.	Num.	Pct.	Num.	Pct.
1987	8,193	5,518	67.3%	2,676	32.7%	100.0%	285	10.7%	1,724	64.4%	283	10.6%	309	11.5%	65	2.4%
1988	8,321	5,733	68.9%	2,588	31.1%	100.0%	235	9.1%	1,759	68.0%	271	10.5%	244	9.4%	72	2.8%
1989	8,400	5,891	70.1%	2,510	29.9%	100.0%	227	9.0%	1,744	69.5%	272	10.8%	186	7.4%	81	3.2%
1990	8,745	6,108	69.8%	2,637	30.2%	100.0%	286	10.9%	1,831	69.5%	276	10.5%	160	6.1%	83	3.2%
1991	9,031	6,205	68.7%	2,826	31.3%	100.0%	243	8.6%	1,928	68.2%	315	11.1%	245	8.7%	95	3.4%
1992	9,567	6,433	67.2%	3,135	32.8%	100.0%	364	11.6%	2,011	64.2%	398	12.7%	278	8.9%	84	2.7%
1993	9,860	6,717	68.1%	3,144	31.9%	100.0%	434	13.8%	1,960	62.4%	443	14.1%	225	7.1%	77	2.5%
1994	9,837	7,022	71.4%	2,815	28.6%	100.0%	470	16.7%	1,626	57.8%	462	16.4%	177	6.3%	79	2.8%
1995	9,887	7,220	73.0%	2,667	27.0%	100.0%	491	18.4%	1,531	57.4%	400	15.0%	163	6.1%	81	3.0%
1996	10,052	7,548	75.1%	2,504	24.9%	100.0%	501	20.0%	1,349	53.9%	375	15.0%	183	7.3%	97	3.9%
1997	9,874	7,636	77.3%	2,238	22.7%	100.0%	446	19.9%	1,197	53.5%	331	14.8%	164	7.3%	100	4.5%
1998	9,881	7,868	79.6%	2,013	20.4%	100.0%	419	20.8%	1,038	51.5%	361	17.9%	113	5.6%	83	4.1%
1999	9,741	7,986	82.0%	1,755	18.0%	100.0%	444	25.3%	875	49.9%	311	17.7%	55	3.1%	67	3.8%
2000	9,712	8,030	82.7%	1,682	17.3%	100.0%	442	26.3%	911	54.2%	223	13.3%	48	2.9%	57	3.4%
2001	10,044	8,148	81.1%	1,896	18.9%	100.0%	527	27.8%	974	51.4%	228	12.0%	89	4.7%	78	4.1%
2002	10,206	8,193	80.3%	2,013	19.7%	100.0%	540	26.8%	989	49.1%	285	14.1%	116	5.8%	83	4.1%
2003	10,411	8,191	78.7%	2,220	21.3%	100.0%	574	25.8%	1,093	49.2%	351	15.8%	130	5.9%	73	3.3%

Year	Total	Worked		Did Not Work During the Year—Primary Reason for Not Working													
				Total			Ill or Disabled		Taking Care of Home or Family		Attending School		Could Not Find Work		Retired or Other	
		Num.	Pct.	Num.	Pct.	Sub-total Pct.	Num.	Pct.	Num.	Pct.	Num.	Pct.	Num.	Pct.	Num.	Pct.
2004	10,442	8,110	77.7%	2,332	22.3%	100.0%	614	26.3%	1,176	50.4%	328	14.1%	133	5.7%	80	3.4%
2005	10,476	8,124	77.6%	2,352	22.4%	100.0%	616	26.2%	1,257	53.4%	292	12.4%	98	4.2%	90	3.8%
2006	10,938	8,458	77.3%	2,479	22.7%	100.0%	689	27.8%	1,245	50.2%	342	13.8%	96	3.9%	108	4.4%
2007	10,748	8,372	77.9%	2,376	22.1%	100.0%	633	26.6%	1,248	52.5%	283	11.9%	95	4.0%	118	5.0%
2008	10,797	8,301	76.9%	2,496	23.1%	100.0%	650	26.0%	1,243	49.8%	356	14.2%	157	6.3%	90	3.6%
2009	10,990	8,133	74.0%	2,856	26.0%	100.0%	679	23.8%	1,292	45.2%	398	13.9%	382	13.4%	105	3.7%
Did Not Receive Cash Welfare																
1987	5,288	4,511	85.3%	778	14.7%	100.0%	84	10.7%	456	58.7%	124	16.0%	75	9.7%	28	3.6%
1988	5,402	4,651	86.1%	751	13.9%	100.0%	74	9.8%	427	56.8%	134	17.9%	58	7.7%	52	7.0%
1989	5,683	4,930	86.7%	754	13.3%	100.0%	75	10.0%	492	65.2%	100	13.2%	42	5.6%	45	5.9%
1990	5,664	4,945	87.3%	719	12.7%	100.0%	67	9.3%	469	65.2%	90	12.6%	39	5.4%	54	7.5%
1991	5,735	5,005	87.3%	730	12.7%	100.0%	69	9.4%	454	62.2%	98	13.4%	72	9.8%	38	5.2%
1992	6,022	5,146	85.4%	876	14.6%	100.0%	102	11.7%	508	58.0%	155	17.7%	71	8.1%	40	4.6%
1993	6,103	5,237	85.8%	866	14.2%	100.0%	124	14.3%	490	56.6%	157	18.1%	45	5.2%	45	5.2%
1994	6,367	5,549	87.2%	817	12.8%	100.0%	130	15.9%	445	54.4%	171	20.9%	38	4.6%	34	4.2%
1995	6,640	5,798	87.3%	842	12.7%	100.0%	119	14.2%	473	56.2%	150	17.8%	53	6.3%	46	5.5%
1996	6,976	6,118	87.7%	858	12.3%	100.0%	108	12.6%	463	54.0%	173	20.2%	66	7.7%	48	5.6%
1997	7,228	6,313	87.3%	916	12.7%	100.0%	121	13.2%	516	56.4%	160	17.4%	60	6.6%	59	6.5%
1998	7,616	6,628	87.0%	989	13.0%	100.0%	162	16.4%	523	52.8%	204	20.6%	42	4.3%	58	5.9%
1999	7,791	6,859	88.0%	933	12.0%	100.0%	172	18.5%	499	53.5%	174	18.7%	31	3.3%	54	5.8%

Table C-16. (Continued)

Year	Total	Worked		Did Not Work During the Year—Primary Reason for Not Working													
				Total			Ill or Disabled		Taking Care of Home or Family		Attending School		Could Not Find Work		Retired or Other	
		Num.	Pct.	Num.	Pct.	Sub-total Pct.	Num.	Pct.	Num.	Pct.	Num.	Pct.	Num.	Pct.	Num.	Pct.
2000	8,065	7,105	88.1%	961	11.9%	100.0%	176	18.3%	558	58.1%	159	16.6%	22	2.3%	46	4.7%
2001	8,520	7,342	86.2%	1,178	13.8%	100.0%	216	18.3%	655	55.6%	175	14.9%	66	5.6%	67	5.7%
2002	8,741	7,453	85.3%	1,288	14.7%	100.0%	234	18.2%	709	55.0%	212	16.5%	61	4.8%	71	5.5%
2003	8,738	7,397	84.7%	1,341	15.3%	100.0%	230	17.1%	726	54.2%	242	18.1%	86	6.4%	56	4.2%
2004	8,850	7,334	82.9%	1,516	17.1%	100.0%	305	20.1%	818	54.0%	241	15.9%	86	5.7%	66	4.3%
2005	8,859	7,379	83.3%	1,480	16.7%	100.0%	275	18.5%	881	59.5%	214	14.5%	48	3.3%	62	4.2%
2006	9,411	7,723	82.1%	1,688	17.9%	100.0%	354	21.0%	910	53.9%	266	15.8%	67	4.0%	90	5.3%
2007	9,329	7,693	82.5%	1,636	17.5%	100.0%	300	18.4%	946	57.8%	225	13.8%	62	3.8%	103	6.3%
2008	9,290	7,545	81.2%	1,745	18.8%	100.0%	341	19.5%	929	53.2%	298	17.1%	102	5.8%	76	4.3%
2009	9,463	7,486	79.1%	1,976	20.9%	100.0%	346	17.5%	939	47.5%	312	15.8%	290	14.7%	89	4.5%
Received Cash Welfare (AFDC/TANF/GA or SSI)																
1987	2,812	972	34.6%	1,839	65.4%	100.0%	187	10.2%	1,237	67.3%	152	8.2%	228	12.4%	35	1.9%
1988	2,828	1,031	36.4%	1,797	63.6%	100.0%	149	8.3%	1,310	72.9%	136	7.5%	185	10.3%	17	1.0%
1989	2,627	906	34.5%	1,721	65.5%	100.0%	147	8.5%	1,236	71.8%	167	9.7%	138	8.0%	34	2.0%
1990	2,991	1,117	37.4%	1,874	62.6%	100.0%	202	10.8%	1,341	71.6%	181	9.7%	120	6.4%	30	1.6%
1991	3,199	1,155	36.1%	2,043	63.9%	100.0%	162	7.9%	1,450	71.0%	210	10.3%	172	8.4%	51	2.5%
1992	3,423	1,229	35.9%	2,193	64.1%	100.0%	232	10.6%	1,480	67.5%	240	10.9%	199	9.1%	43	1.9%
1993	3,598	1,388	38.6%	2,210	61.4%	100.0%	275	12.4%	1,449	65.6%	279	12.6%	175	7.9%	32	1.4%
1994	3,318	1,395	42.0%	1,924	58.0%	100.0%	305	15.8%	1,149	59.7%	288	15.0%	137	7.1%	44	2.3%
1995	3,055	1,326	43.4%	1,729	56.6%	100.0%	324	18.7%	1,019	58.9%	247	14.3%	108	6.3%	31	1.8%

Year	Total	Worked		Did Not Work During the Year—Primary Reason for Not Working													
				Total			Ill or Disabled		Taking Care of Home or Family		Attending School		Could Not Find Work		Retired or Other	
		Num.	Pct.	Num.	Pct.	Sub-total Pct.	Num.	Pct.	Num.	Pct.	Num.	Pct.	Num.	Pct.	Num.	Pct.
1996	2,872	1,317	45.9%	1,555	54.1%	100.0%	343	22.1%	849	54.6%	200	12.9%	115	7.4%	47	3.0%
1997	2,436	1,212	49.8%	1,224	50.2%	100.0%	270	22.1%	654	53.4%	160	13.0%	102	8.3%	38	3.1%
1998	2,069	1,147	55.4%	922	44.6%	100.0%	196	21.3%	486	52.7%	153	16.6%	68	7.4%	19	2.0%
1999	1,747	1,017	58.2%	730	41.8%	100.0%	226	30.9%	341	46.7%	131	17.9%	19	2.6%	13	1.8%
2000	1,431	812	56.7%	619	43.3%	100.0%	205	33.1%	322	51.9%	58	9.4%	24	3.8%	10	1.7%
2001	1,294	679	52.5%	615	47.5%	100.0%	244	39.7%	291	47.4%	49	8.0%	20	3.3%	10	1.6%
2002	1,245	645	51.9%	599	48.1%	100.0%	224	37.3%	245	41.0%	67	11.3%	53	8.8%	10	1.6%
2003	1,463	704	48.1%	759	51.9%	100.0%	262	34.5%	344	45.3%	98	13.0%	41	5.4%	15	2.0%
2004	1,323	646	48.8%	677	51.2%	100.0%	228	33.6%	321	47.4%	73	10.7%	46	6.7%	10	1.5%
2005	1,359	631	46.5%	728	53.5%	100.0%	261	35.9%	327	45.0%	72	9.8%	46	6.3%	21	2.9%
2006	1,259	609	48.4%	649	51.6%	100.0%	247	38.0%	296	45.5%	67	10.3%	27	4.2%	13	2.0%
2007	1,149	560	48.8%	588	51.2%	100.0%	240	40.8%	254	43.1%	53	9.0%	28	4.8%	13	2.2%
2008	1,241	628	50.6%	613	49.4%	100.0%	224	36.5%	281	45.7%	50	8.1%	47	7.7%	12	1.9%
2009	1,247	522	41.9%	725	58.1%	100.0%	249	34.4%	305	42.1%	72	10.0%	84	11.6%	14	1.9%
Received AFDC/TANF/GA Only																
1987	2,493	887	35.6%	1,606	64.4%	100.0%	111	6.9%	1,117	69.6%	138	8.6%	212	13.2%	26	1.6%
1988	2,536	935	36.9%	1,600	63.1%	100.0%	88	5.5%	1,200	75.0%	133	8.3%	164	10.2%	15	0.9%
1989	2,313	817	35.3%	1,496	64.7%	100.0%	92	6.2%	1,113	74.4%	147	9.8%	121	8.1%	23	1.5%
1990	2,651	1,013	38.2%	1,638	61.8%	100.0%	106	6.5%	1,235	75.4%	164	10.0%	109	6.6%	25	1.5%
1991	2,822	1,036	36.7%	1,786	63.3%	100.0%	90	5.0%	1,308	73.3%	190	10.6%	157	8.8%	41	2.3%

Table C-16. (Continued)

Year	Total	Worked		Did Not Work During the Year—Primary Reason for Not Working												
				Total			Ill or Disabled		Taking Care of Home or Family		Attending School		Could Not Find Work		Retired or Other	
		Num.	Pct.	Num.	Pct.	Sub-total Pct.	Num.	Pct.	Num.	Pct.	Num.	Pct.	Num.	Pct.	Num.	Pct.
1992	2,990	1,095	36.6%	1,895	63.4%	100.0%	133	7.0%	1,331	70.3%	221	11.7%	172	9.1%	37	2.0%
1993	3,010	1,198	39.8%	1,812	60.2%	100.0%	145	8.0%	1,248	68.9%	240	13.2%	153	8.4%	26	1.4%
1994	2,745	1,228	44.7%	1,517	55.3%	100.0%	124	8.1%	994	65.5%	247	16.3%	117	7.7%	37	2.4%
1995	2,525	1,157	45.8%	1,368	54.2%	100.0%	156	11.4%	859	62.8%	230	16.8%	99	7.2%	24	1.8%
1996	2,321	1,129	48.7%	1,191	51.3%	100.0%	157	13.2%	699	58.7%	179	15.1%	111	9.3%	45	3.7%
1997	1,923	1,017	52.9%	906	47.1%	100.0%	106	11.7%	539	59.5%	131	14.5%	94	10.4%	36	3.9%
1998	1,604	984	61.3%	620	38.7%	100.0%	61	9.9%	374	60.4%	118	19.0%	56	9.1%	10	1.7%
1999	1,331	839	63.0%	492	37.0%	100.0%	96	19.4%	267	54.3%	107	21.7%	12	2.4%	11	2.2%
2000	1,033	642	62.1%	391	37.9%	100.0%	60	15.3%	256	65.5%	49	12.5%	20	5.1%	6	1.6%
2001	894	516	57.8%	377	42.2%	100.0%	80	21.3%	229	60.6%	42	11.2%	18	4.7%	8	2.1%
2002	874	500	57.2%	374	42.8%	100.0%	72	19.2%	192	51.5%	57	15.2%	45	12.1%	7	2.0%
2003	1,073	568	52.9%	505	47.1%	100.0%	95	18.8%	296	58.6%	75	14.9%	27	5.4%	12	2.4%
2004	888	481	54.1%	407	45.9%	100.0%	61	15.1%	253	62.1%	53	13.0%	35	8.7%	4	1.0%
2005	917	486	53.0%	431	47.0%	100.0%	93	21.6%	233	54.1%	63	14.5%	32	7.4%	10	2.3%
2006	833	456	54.7%	377	45.3%	100.0%	92	24.5%	207	54.8%	49	12.9%	21	5.4%	9	2.3%
2007	751	417	55.6%	334	44.4%	100.0%	81	24.3%	177	53.0%	44	13.2%	21	6.3%	11	3.3%
2008	844	467	55.3%	377	44.7%	100.0%	76	20.1%	219	58.2%	42	11.1%	32	8.4%	8	2.2%
2009	811	360	44.4%	451	55.6%	100.0%	91	20.2%	228	50.4%	52	11.4%	69	15.3%	11	2.5%
Received SSI Only																
1987	93	35	37.4%	58	62.6%	100.0%	15	25.5%	30	51.4%	7	12.1%	5	8.9%	1	2.0%

Year	Total	Worked		Did Not Work During the Year—Primary Reason for Not Working													
				Total			Ill or Disabled		Taking Care of Home or Family		Attending School		Could Not Find Work		Retired or Other	
		Num.	Pct.	Num.	Pct.	Sub-total Pct.	Num.	Pct.	Num.	Pct.	Num.	Pct.	Num.	Pct.	Num.	Pct.
1988	91	52	57.0%	39	43.0%	100.0%	13	33.7%	22	55.3%	1	2.7%	1	2.0%	2	6.2%
1989	90	55	61.5%	35	38.5%	100.0%	5	14.3%	17	47.7%	5	15.7%	5	15.0%	3	7.3%
1990	90	45	50.6%	44	49.4%	100.0%	18	39.7%	22	49.0%	5	10.5%	0	0.8%	0	0.0%
1991	98	45	46.3%	52	53.7%	100.0%	13	25.0%	24	45.8%	7	14.1%	2	2.9%	6	12.2%
1992	122	57	46.8%	65	53.2%	100.0%	30	45.9%	23	35.4%	2	3.8%	8	12.7%	1	2.3%
1993	159	92	57.6%	68	42.4%	100.0%	35	51.5%	21	31.4%	7	9.7%	4	5.9%	1	1.5%
1994	152	78	51.5%	74	48.5%	100.0%	35	47.1%	32	44.0%	3	4.6%	2	2.9%	1	1.5%
1995	193	96	50.0%	96	50.0%	100.0%	48	50.2%	39	40.7%	3	3.3%	2	1.9%	4	4.0%
1996	203	113	55.4%	91	44.6%	100.0%	50	54.8%	37	40.6%	1	1.4%	2	1.7%	1	1.5%
1997	210	112	53.0%	99	47.0%	100.0%	56	56.2%	27	27.5%	12	11.7%	2	1.9%	3	2.7%
1998	196	94	47.7%	103	52.3%	100.0%	61	59.1%	29	28.6%	4	4.1%	2	1.8%	7	6.4%
1999	203	111	54.7%	92	45.3%	100.0%	47	50.7%	35	37.7%	6	6.3%	5	5.2%	0	0.0%
2000	216	114	52.7%	102	47.3%	100.0%	61	59.8%	32	30.9%	6	5.5%	2	2.3%	2	1.5%
2001	230	127	54.9%	104	45.1%	100.0%	68	65.1%	28	27.0%	4	3.9%	2	2.3%	2	1.8%
2002	220	94	42.7%	126	57.3%	100.0%	83	65.5%	34	27.2%	5	3.9%	2	1.4%	2	2.0%
2003	210	90	42.7%	121	57.3%	100.0%	83	68.5%	22	18.7%	11	8.9%	3	2.5%	2	1.5%
2004	269	131	48.6%	138	51.4%	100.0%	82	59.0%	37	26.9%	14	10.0%	2	1.2%	4	2.9%
2005	258	114	44.2%	144	55.8%	100.0%	80	55.5%	48	33.6%	6	4.1%	3	2.3%	7	4.6%
2006	268	126	47.0%	142	53.0%	100.0%	89	62.4%	38	27.0%	9	6.4%	1	1.0%	4	3.1%
2007	271	119	44.0%	152	56.0%	100.0%	93	61.0%	48	31.6%	5	3.3%	4	2.7%	2	1.4%

Table C-16. (Continued)

Year	Total	Worked		Did Not Work During the Year—Primary Reason for Not Working												
				Total			Ill or Disabled		Taking Care of Home or Family		Attending School		Could Not Find Work		Retired or Other	
		Num.	Pct.	Num.	Pct.	Sub-total Pct.	Num.	Pct.	Num.	Pct.	Num.	Pct.	Num.	Pct.	Num.	Pct.
2008	267	129	48.3%	138	51.7%	100.0%	85	61.8%	34	24.6%	8	5.9%	8	5.8%	3	1.9%
2009	280	125	44.5%	155	55.5%	100.0%	84	54.0%	48	30.7%	14	8.8%	8	4.9%	2	1.6%
Received AFDC/TANF/GA and SSI																
1987	226	51	22.4%	175	77.6%	100.0%	61	34.7%	90	51.2%	6	3.5%	11	6.1%	8	4.4%
1988	201	43	21.5%	158	78.5%	100.0%	47	29.8%	89	56.2%	1	0.7%	21	13.3%	0	0.0%
1989	224	34	15.0%	191	85.0%	100.0%	50	26.0%	106	55.7%	14	7.3%	13	6.6%	8	4.4%
1990	251	59	23.5%	192	76.5%	100.0%	78	40.7%	85	44.1%	13	6.6%	11	6.0%	5	2.7%
1991	279	74	26.5%	205	73.5%	100.0%	59	28.6%	118	57.3%	13	6.1%	13	6.4%	3	1.5%
1992	311	77	24.8%	234	75.2%	100.0%	69	29.5%	126	53.8%	17	7.1%	19	8.0%	4	1.5%
1993	429	99	23.0%	331	77.0%	100.0%	95	28.7%	180	54.4%	33	9.9%	19	5.6%	5	1.5%
1994	421	89	21.1%	333	78.9%	100.0%	146	44.0%	123	37.0%	38	11.5%	19	5.6%	6	1.9%
1995	337	73	21.6%	264	78.4%	100.0%	119	45.0%	121	45.8%	14	5.3%	7	2.7%	3	1.2%
1996	348	75	21.6%	273	78.4%	100.0%	137	50.1%	113	41.3%	19	7.1%	3	1.1%	1	0.4%
1997	302	83	27.5%	219	72.5%	100.0%	109	49.7%	87	39.7%	17	7.8%	6	2.8%	0	0.0%
1998	268	69	25.8%	199	74.2%	100.0%	74	37.4%	82	41.2%	31	15.4%	10	5.2%	2	0.8%
1999	213	66	31.2%	146	68.8%	100.0%	83	57.0%	39	26.9%	19	12.7%	2	1.7%	2	1.6%
2000	183	57	31.0%	126	69.0%	100.0%	84	66.9%	34	26.9%	4	3.0%	2	1.2%	2	1.9%
2001	170	37	21.5%	133	78.5%	100.0%	96	72.0%	34	25.9%	3	2.0%	0	0.2%	0	0.0%
2002	151	51	33.9%	100	66.1%	100.0%	69	69.3%	19	18.8%	6	5.7%	6	6.1%	0	0.0%
2003	180	46	25.5%	134	74.5%	100.0%	84	62.9%	26	19.2%	12	9.2%	11	7.9%	1	0.8%

Year	Total	Worked		Did Not Work During the Year—Primary Reason for Not Working												
				Total			Ill or Disabled		Taking Care of Home or Family		Attending School		Could Not Find Work		Retired or Other	
		Num.	Pct.	Num.	Pct.	Sub-total Pct.	Num.	Pct.	Num.	Pct.	Num.	Pct.	Num.	Pct.	Num.	Pct.
2004	167	35	20.8%	132	79.2%	100.0%	84	64.1%	31	23.5%	6	4.4%	8	6.4%	2	1.6%
2005	184	31	16.9%	153	83.1%	100.0%	89	57.9%	46	29.8%	3	2.0%	11	7.0%	5	3.3%
2006	158	28	17.6%	130	82.4%	100.0%	66	50.5%	50	38.8%	9	6.8%	5	3.8%	0	0.0%
2007	126	24	18.7%	103	81.3%	100.0%	66	64.5%	29	28.3%	4	4.1%	3	3.1%	0	0.0%
2008	130	32	24.4%	99	75.6%	100.0%	63	63.9%	27	27.8%	0	0.0%	7	7.5%	1	0.8%
2009	156	38	24.2%	119	75.8%	100.0%	74	62.7%	30	25.1%	7	5.8%	8	6.4%	0	0.0%

Source: Congressional Research Service (CRS) estimates based on analysis of U.S. Census Bureau 1988 to 2010 Current Population Survey (CPS) Annual Social and Economic Supplement (ASEC) data.

Note: Support table for Figure 17 and Figure 18.

Table C-17. Single Mothers' Job Attachment, 1987 to 2009 (Numbers in 1,000s)

Year	Total	Worked During the Year								Did Not Work During the Year					
		Total		Worked Full-Time, Full-Year		Worked LessThan Full-Time, Full-Year, Due toUnemployment orDiscouragement		Worked LessThan Full-Time, Full-Year, forPersonalReasons		Total		Did NotWork Due to Unemploy-ment or Discourage-ment		Did NotWork Due to PersonalReasons	
		Num.	Pct.	Num.	Pct.	Num.	Pct.	Num.	Pct.	Num.	Pct.	Num.	Pct.	Num.	Pct.
1987	8,193	5,518	67.3%	2,636	32.2%	1,296	15.8%	1,586	19.4%	2,676	32.7%	449	5.5%	2,217	27.1%
1988	8,321	5,733	68.9%	2,809	33.8%	1,299	15.6%	1,625	19.5%	2,588	31.1%	434	5.2%	2,147	25.8%
1989	8,400	5,891	70.1%	2,810	33.4%	1,325	15.8%	1,756	20.9%	2,510	29.9%	324	3.9%	2,185	26.0%
1990	8,745	6,108	69.8%	2,815	32.2%	1,461	16.7%	1,825	20.9%	2,637	30.2%	343	3.9%	2,294	26.2%
1991	9,031	6,205	68.7%	2,925	32.4%	1,569	17.4%	1,709	18.9%	2,826	31.3%	427	4.7%	2,399	26.6%
1992	9,567	6,433	67.2%	3,030	31.7%	1,668	17.4%	1,735	18.1%	3,135	32.8%	468	4.9%	2,666	27.9%
1993	9,860	6,717	68.1%	3,143	31.9%	1,695	17.2%	1,871	19.0%	3,144	31.9%	557	5.7%	2,582	26.2%
1994	9,837	7,022	71.4%	3,259	33.1%	1,720	17.5%	2,038	20.7%	2,815	28.6%	442	4.5%	2,372	24.1%
1995	9,887	7,220	73.0%	3,589	36.3%	1,609	16.3%	2,020	20.4%	2,667	27.0%	406	4.1%	2,261	22.9%
1996	10,052	7,548	75.1%	3,646	36.3%	1,693	16.8%	2,200	21.9%	2,504	24.9%	425	4.2%	2,079	20.7%
1997	9,874	7,636	77.3%	3,838	38.9%	1,568	15.9%	2,225	22.5%	2,238	22.7%	362	3.7%	1,877	19.0%
1998	9,881	7,868	79.6%	4,116	41.7%	1,543	15.6%	2,200	22.3%	2,013	20.4%	270	2.7%	1,744	17.6%
1999	9,741	7,986	82.0%	4,286	44.0%	1,428	14.7%	2,269	23.3%	1,755	18.0%	151	1.5%	1,602	16.4%
2000	9,712	8,030	82.7%	4,459	45.9%	1,251	12.9%	2,307	23.8%	1,682	17.3%	174	1.8%	1,508	15.5%
2001	10,044	8,148	81.1%	4,505	44.9%	1,492	14.9%	2,138	21.3%	1,896	18.9%	193	1.9%	1,701	16.9%
2002	10,206	8,193	80.3%	4,649	45.6%	1,556	15.2%	1,980	19.4%	2,013	19.7%	271	2.7%	1,742	17.1%

Year	Total	Worked During the Year								Did Not Work During the Year					
		Total		Worked Full-Time, Full-Year		Worked LessThan Full-Time, Full-Year, Due toUnemployment orDiscouragement		Worked LessThan Full-Time, Full-Year, forPersonalReasons		Total		Did NotWork Due to Unemploy-ment or Discourage-ment		Did NotWork Due to PersonalReasons	
		Num.	Pct.	Num.	Pct.	Num.	Pct.	Num.	Pct.	Num.	Pct.	Num.	Pct.	Num.	Pct.
2003	10,411	8,191	78.7%	4,569	43.9%	1,575	15.1%	2,040	19.6%	2,220	21.3%	297	2.8%	1,924	18.5%
2004	10,442	8,110	77.7%	4,476	42.9%	1,497	14.3%	2,134	20.4%	2,332	22.3%	294	2.8%	2,038	19.5%
2005	10,476	8,124	77.6%	4,657	44.5%	1,398	13.3%	2,060	19.7%	2,352	22.4%	249	2.4%	2,102	20.1%
2006	10,938	8,458	77.3%	4,845	44.3%	1,452	13.3%	2,156	19.7%	2,479	22.7%	233	2.1%	2,245	20.5%
2007	10,748	8,372	77.9%	4,702	43.8%	1,519	14.1%	2,142	19.9%	2,376	22.1%	229	2.1%	2,146	20.0%
2008	10,797	8,301	76.9%	4,426	41.0%	1,989	18.4%	1,882	17.4%	2,496	23.1%	281	2.6%	2,212	20.5%
2009	10,990	8,133	74.0%	4,252	38.7%	2,041	18.6%	1,832	16.7%	2,856	26.0%	569	5.2%	2,285	20.8%

Source: Congressional Research Service (CRS) estimates based on analysis of U.S. Census Bureau 1988 to 2010 Current Population Survey (CPS) Annual Social and Economic Supplement (ASEC) data.

Notes: Persons who worked for 50 weeks or more and 35 or more hours per week are designated as full-time, full-year workers. Unemployed are persons who were without a job and searched for work. Discouraged workers are persons who were without a job but did not search for work because they believed no jobs were available. Personal reasons for not working during the year, or working less than full-time, full-year, include taking care of home or family, attending school, illness or disability, retired, or other.

Support table for Figure 20.

End Notes

[1] Most data presented in this report are based on CRS analysis of 23 years of data from the U.S. Census Bureau's Annual Social and Economic Supplement to the Current Population Survey (CPS/ASEC). The CPS/ASEC is the principal source for annual income, poverty, and health insurance coverage estimates issued by the Census Bureau. The annual survey is a supplement to the monthly CPS conducted for the U.S. Bureau of Labor Statistics (BLS) used in deriving monthly labor force statistics, such as the national unemployment rate. Estimates from the annual supplement, conducted in February through April, represent characteristics at the time of the survey, and income, poverty, and health insurance status in the previous year. The analysis is limited to survey data collected from 1988 through 2010 (the most recent available), representing income and poverty status from 1987 through 2009. The CPS/ASEC analysis in this report is limited to the past 23 years due to relative consistency in design and content of the CPS/ASEC over the period.

[2] See, for example, Catherine Rampell, "'Great Recession': A Brief Etymology," *New York Times* (internet edition), March 11, 2009, available at http://economix.blogs.nytimes.com/ 2009/03/11/great-recession-a-brief-etymology/.

[3] Single fathers and their children have received comparative little study, nor have they emerged as a matter of policy concern, as have single mothers and their children.

[4] The official U.S. statistical poverty measure is based on families' annual pre-tax income relative to family poverty income thresholds, which vary by family size and composition. For example, in 2009, a family consisting of a single mother with one child was considered poor if its annual pre-tax cash income was less than $14,787, and if she had two children, she and her children would be considered poor if her family income was below $17,285. In turn, a married couple with one child would be considered poor if the family's income was less than $17,268, and if they had two children, if its income was less than $21,756.

[5] The definition of "children" used here represents dependent children under the age of 18 who are related to another family member by birth or adoption. It excludes children who are unrelated to other household members, and excludes persons under the age of 18 who themselves have a dependent child residing with them.

[6] James T. Patterson, *America's Struggle Against Poverty, 1900-1985* (Cambridge, MA: Harvard University Press, 1986), p. 179.

[7] Section 1115 of the Social Security Act grants the Secretary authority to waive compliance of states with certain sections of the Social Security Act for state experiments or demonstrations that the Secretary judges to promote specific objectives of the act.

[8] Economic recessions are defined by the National Bureau of Economic Research (NBER) Business Cycle Dating Committee.

[9] For analyses of AFDC caseload growth over this period, see CRS Report 93-7, *Demographic Trends Affecting Aid to Families with Dependent Children (AFDC) Caseload Growth*, by Thomas Gabe (archived report, available to congressional clients upon request); also, Janice Peskin, Forecasting AFDC Caseloads, with an Emphasis on Economic Factors, Congressional Budget Office Staff Memorandum, July 1993; and, Rebecca Blank, "What Causes Public Assistance Caseloads to Grow?," *Journal of Human Resources*, vol. 36, no. 1 (Winter 2001), pp. 85-118.

[10] Available at http://frwebgate.access.gpo.gov/cgi-bin/getdoc.cgi?dbname=1992_public_papers_ vol1_text&docid= pap_text-79.pdf.

[11] Gwen Ifill, "Clinton Presses Welfare Overhaul, Stressing Job Training and Work," *New York Times*, September 10, 1992, pp. A1, A19.

[12] Richard L. Berke, "The Ad Campaign—Clinton: Getting People Off Welfare," *New York Times*, September 10, 1992, p. A-19.

[13] "House GOP Offers Descriptions Of Bills To Enact 'Contract'." In CQ Almanac 1994, 50th ed., 39-D-52-D. Washington, DC: Congressional Quarterly, 1995, http://library.cqpress.com/ cqalmanac/cqal94-843-25141-1102086.

[14] "Welfare Reform," in *Contract with America : the bold plan by Rep. Newt Gingrich, Rep. Dick Armey and the House Republicans to change the nation*, ed. Ed Gillespie and Bob Schellhas (New York: Times Books, 1994), p. 65.

[15] Federal Insurance Contributions Act taxes.

[16] A state's work participation requirement may be reduced for specified reasons (e.g., reductions in a state's caseload "caseload reduction credit," or states spent more than that required by TANF's MOE). See CRS Report RL32760, *The Temporary Assistance for Needy Families (TANF) Block Grant: Responses to Frequently Asked Questions*, by Gene Falk.

[17] Up to 20% of the TANF caseload can be extended to receive assistance beyond five years due to "hardship," as defined by the states. See CRS Report RL32748, *The Temporary Assistance for Needy Families (TANF) Block Grant: A Primer on TANF Financing and Federal Requirements*, by Gene Falk.

[18] See, for example, the Urban Institute's Welfare Rules Database, on the Internet at http://anfdata.urban.org/wrd/ WRDWelcome.cfm.

[19] For a discussion of changes in work incentives under TANF compared to AFDC, see CRS Report RL30579, *Welfare Reform: Financial Eligibility Rules and Cash Assistance Amounts under TANF*, by Craig Abbey (archived report, available upon request).

[20] Maximum TANF benefits available for a family of three in the median state in July 2008 were 36% below the maximum level available to a family under AFDC in July 1988, after adjusting for the effects of price inflation. In July 1988, the maximum benefit level in the median state amounted to 45% of the Department of Health and Human Services Federal Poverty Guidelines (FPL), but by 2008, only 29%. In 1988, the maximum benefit ranged from a low of 14.6% of FPL (Alabama) to 82.1% of FPL (California). By 2008, the maximum benefit ranged from a low of 11.6% of FPL (Mississippi) to a high of 50.3% of FPL (Alaska). Author's estimates based on data from U.S. Congress, House Committee on Ways and Means, *2008 Green Book*, Section 7—Temporary Assistance for Needy Families, 111th Cong., Table 7-22, pp. 49-50, available on the internet at http://waysandmeans.house.gov/media/pdf/110/tanf.pdf; and Gretchen Rowe and Mary Murphy, Welfare Rules Databook: State TANF Policies as of July 2008, The Urban Institute, Washington, DC, August 2009, Table L5, Maximum Monthly Benefit for A Family of Three with No income, August 2009, pp. 184-185, http://anfdata.urban.org/ databooks/Databook%202008%20FINAL.pdf.

[21] See CRS Report RL32760, *The Temporary Assistance for Needy Families (TANF) Block Grant: Responses to Frequently Asked Questions*, by Gene Falk.

[22] The federal minimum wage increased from $3.35 per hour to $3.80 per hour, effective April 1990, to $4.25 per hour, effective April 1991, to $4.75 per hour, effective October 1996, $5.15 per hour, effective September 1997, $5.85 per hour, effective July 2007, and $6.65 per hour, effective July 2008. In July 2009, the minimum wage was increased to $7.25 per hour. For an analysis of possible effects of minimum wage increases on welfare participation, see Mark Turner, *The Effects of Minimum Wages on Welfare Recipiency*, paper presented at the National Association for Welfare Research and Statistics, August 1998.

[23] U.S. Department of Labor, Wage and Hour Division, *Changes in Basic Minimum Wages in Non-Farm Employment Under State Law: Selected Years 1968 to 2011*, http://www.dol.gov /whd/state/stateMinWageHis.htm.

[24] For tax year 2010 see Erica Williams, Nicholas Johnson, and Jon Shure, *State Earned Income Tax Credits: 2010 Legislative Update*, Center for Budget and Policy Priorities, December 9, 2010, http://www.cbpp.org/cms/index.cfm? fa=view&id=2987. For earlier tax years, see http://www.taxpolicycenter.org/taxfacts/Content/Excel/state_eitc.xls.

[25] This section is based on CRS Report RS22380, *Child Support Enforcement: Program Basics*, by Carmen Solomon-Fears; CRS Report RL34203, *Child Support Enforcement Program Incentive Payments: Background and Policy Issues*, by Carmen Solomon-Fears; and, CRS Report R41431, *Child Well-Being and Noncustodial Fathers*, by Carmen Solomon-Fears, Gene Falk, and Adrienne L. Fernandes-Alcantara.

[26] The federal government reimburses each state 66% of all allowable expenditures on CSE activities. The federal government's funding is "open-ended" in that it pays its percentage of expenditures by matching the amounts spent by state and local governments with no upper limit or ceiling. The federal government also provides incentive payments to states to encourage them to operate effective programs. Federal law requires states to reinvest CSE incentive payments back into the CSE program or related activities. In addition to state and federal matching funds and incentive payments, states collect child support on behalf of families receiving AFDC/TANF to reimburse themselves (and the federal government) for the cost of AFDC/TANF cash payments to the family. Federal law requires families who receive AFDC/TANF cash assistance to assign their child support rights to the state in order to receive AFDC/TANF. In addition, such families must cooperate with the state if necessary to establish paternity and secure child support. CSE collections on behalf of families receiving AFDC/TANF cash benefits are used to reimburse state and federal governments for AFDC/TANF payments made to the family (i.e., child support payments go to the state instead of the family, except for amounts that states choose to "pass through" to the family as additional income that does not affect TANF eligibility or benefit amounts). Additionally, states may charge application fees and apply recovered costs from nonwelfare families to help finance their CSE programs.

[27] For a discussion of issues and policies and programs relating to this topic see CRS Report RL34756, *Nonmarital Childbearing: Trends, Reasons, and Public Policy Interventions*, by Carmen Solomon-Fears.

[28] The Congressional Budget Office (CBO) projects that it will not be until 2016 that the U.S. unemployment rate will reach 5.3%, near what the agency estimates as the natural rate of unemployment of 5.2% (the rate of unemployment arising from all sources except fluctuations in aggregate demand). See Congressional Budget Office, *The Budget and Economic Outlook: Fiscal Years 2011 to 2021*, January 2011, p. XII, http://www.cbo.gov/ftpdocs/120xx/doc12039/01-26_FY2011Outlook.pdf.

[29] For a discussion see CRS Report RL34715, *The Child Tax Credit*, by Maxim Shvedov.

[30] $3,000 + ($1,000/.15) = $9,667.

[31] $12,550 + ($1,000/.15) = $19,217.

[32] For a thorough discussion of the UI system, see CRS Report RL33362, *Unemployment Insurance: Programs and Benefits*, by Katelin P. Isaacs and Julie M. Whittaker.

[33] EUC08 benefits are fully federally funded out of the federal Unemployment Trust Fund (UTF) and from general funds. Since originally passed into law, authorization for the EUC08 program has been extended a number of times—most recently on December, 17, 2010, when the President signed P.L. 111-312, the Tax Relief, Unemployment Insurance Reauthorization, and Job Creation Act of 2010, which extended the EUC08 program's authorization until January 3, 2012.

[34] See CRS Report R40368, *Unemployment Insurance Provisions in the American Recovery and Reinvestment Act of 2009*, by Alison M. Shelton, and Julie M. Whittaker, and CRS Report RS21356, *Taxation of Unemployment Benefits*, by Julie M. Whittaker.

[35] Other UC programs include unemployment benefits for former U.S. military service members (UCX program), Disaster Unemployment Assistance (DUA) benefits, workers who lose their jobs because of international competition who receive additional or supplemental support through the Trade Adjustment Act (TAA) programs.

[36] See CRS Report R41374, *Reducing SNAP (Food Stamp) Benefits Provided by the ARRA: P.L. 111-226 and P.L. 111-296*, by Joe Richardson, Jim Monke, and Gene Falk.

[37] CRS Report R40211 , *Human Services Provisions of the American Recovery and Reinvestment Act*, by Gene Falk et al (archived). Also see CRS Report R41078, *The TANF Emergency Contingency Fund*, by Gene Falk.

[38] CRS Report R40211, op. cit.

[39] Estimates are for children in female-headed "households," which differs somewhat from the CRS definition of female-headed "families" used later in this report based on analysis of U.S. Census Bureau Current Population Survey (CPS) Annual Social and Economic Supplement (ASEC) data.

[40] See, for example Council of Economic Advisors, *Technical Report: The Effects of Welfare Policy and the Economic Expansion on Welfare Caseloads: An Update*, A Report by the Council of Economic Advisors, Washington, DC, August 1999; James P. Ziliak, David N. Figlio, and Elizabeth E. Davis, et al., "Accounting for the Decline in AFDC Caseloads, Welfare Reform or the Economy?," *The Journal of Human Resources*, vol. XXXV, no. 3, pp. 570-586; Robert A. Moffitt, "The Effect of Pre-PRWORA Waivers on AFDC Caseloads and Female Earnings, Income, and Labor Force Behavior," in *Economic Conditions and Welfare Reform*, ed. Sheldon Danziger (Kalamazoo, Mich.: W.E. Upjohn Institute for Employment Research, 1999); June E. O'Neill and Anne M. Hill, *Gaining Ground? Measuring the Impact of Welfare Reform on Welfare and Work*, Manhattan Institute, Civic Report No. 17, New York, New York, 2001; Caroline Danielson and Jacob Alex Klerman, "Did Welfare Reform Cause the Caseload Decline," *Social Service Review*, vol. 82, no. 4 (December 2008), pp. 703-730.

[41] The CPS/ASEC data groups any General Assistance individuals or families may have received with AFDC and TANF. GA programs are financed and administered at the state, county, or local level, and are generally used to meet the needs of people who are ineligible for federally funded cash assistance (e.g., AFDC/TANF, SSI) or are awaiting approval for such benefits. In 1998, 35 states and the District of Columbia had GA programs. See L. Jerome Gallagher, Cori E. Uccello, and Alicia B. Pierce, et al., *State General Assistance Programs 1998*, The Urban Institute, Assessing the New Federalism, Discussion Paper 99-01, Washington, DC, April 1999, http://www.urban.org/publications/ 409066.html.

[42] See Appendix B, which compares CPS estimates to AFDC/TANF caseload counts.

[43] Administrative caseload statistics show the caseload as peaking in March 1994, with nearly 5.1 million cases. In December 2007, at the onset of the recession, the caseload stood at 1.653 million, or only about one-third the level of its March 1994 peak. By December 2009, the caseload had increased somewhat from that of two years earlier, to 1.860 million, a 12.5% increase.

[44] See Appendix B on CPS under-reporting.

[45] Email exchanges with Census Bureau contacts, relaying the author's findings, have not resulted in an attributable explanation for the sudden dip and recovery of EITC receipt among this subgroup of the population. EITC receipt is not directly reported on the CPS/ASEC. The Census Bureau estimates the EITC and other tax variables on the CPS/ASEC using a tax model. Beginning with the 2004 CPS, the Census Bureau implemented a new tax model, providing new tax estimates for income year 2003. It's uncertain whether model changes may have contributed the sudden aberration in trend of estimated EITC receipt.

[46] For example, a disabled child might qualify for SSI, while the parent could potentially qualify for AFDC, or vice versa if the parent were disabled. For a discussion, see David C. Stapleton, David C. Wittenburg, and Michael E. Fishman, et al., "Transitions from AFDC to SSI Before Welfare Reform," *Social Security Bulletin*, vol. 64, no. 1 (2001), pp. 84-114.

[47] Ibid., p. 86.

[48] As with the EITC, ACTC estimates are Census Bureau model-based estimates.

[49] The order in which income components are added can influence the measured marginal effect of each.

[50] For discussion, see CRS Report R41187, *Poverty Measurement in the United States: History, Current Practice, and Proposed Changes*, by Thomas Gabe. The NAS panel recommended that new means be developed for establishing poverty income thresholds, and that those thresholds be based on distributions of resources families have to spend on the basic necessities of food, clothing, shelter and utilities, plus a little bit more, for other goods and services. Among its recommendations, the NAS panel recommended that in-kind benefits, such as Food Stamps, among others not part of the current "official" poverty definition, be included in the family resource definition, as well as net taxes families pay or net tax credits they receive. Additionally, they recommended that work-related expenses (e.g., child care, work-related transportation) be subtracted from income.

[51] See http://www.esa.doc.gov/news/2010/03/02/census-bureau-develop-supplemental-poverty-measure.

[52] Alaska, California, Connecticut, Minnesota, and Virginia. See Gretchen Rowe, Mary Murphy, and Ei Yin Mon, Welfare Rules Databook: State TANF Policies as of July 2009, The Urban Institute, Washington, DC, August 2010, Table IV.A.5, Maximum Income for Ongoing Eligibility for A Family of Three, July 2009, pp. 140-141 http://anfdata.urban.org/databooks/Databook%202009%20FINAL.pdf.

[53] Note that the value of the EITC on the CPS is based on Census Bureau imputations, rather than actual reported tax credits. Also, the EITC is different from most sources of income, as most families receive the EITC as a lump sum refund at the beginning of year following that in which income used in determining the credit was earned.

[54] In 1993, the after-tax poverty rate (counting Food Stamps/SNAP) among single mothers dropped from 42.7% (line 4) to 41.9% (line 5), a 0.8 percentage point (1.9%) reduction. In 2009, the EITC reduced poverty from 33.5% to 29.6%, a 3.9 percentage point (11.6%) reduction.

[55] CRS estimates from the CPS/ASEC. About 25% of nonworking single mothers, on average, lived in extended families in the pre-TANF era (1987-1996), compared to about 28% in the TANF era.

[56] CRS estimates from the CPS/ASEC. Beginning with the 2007 CPS/ASEC cohabiting couples are identifiable based on self-report. In earlier years, cohabiting couples are identifiable indirectly by inference. The method used here, for CPS/ASEC years before 2007 is based on households with two unmarried adults, who are unrelated and of the opposite sex, and no other adults reside in the household.

[57] Up to 20% of the TANF caseload can be extended to receive assistance beyond five years due to "hardship," as defined by the states. See CRS Report RL32748, *The Temporary Assistance for Needy Families (TANF) Block Grant: A Primer on TANF Financing and Federal Requirements*, by Gene Falk.

[58] Bruce D. Meyer and Dan T. Rosenbaum, "Welfare, the Earned Income Tax Credit, and the Labor Supply of Single Mothers," *Quarterly Journal of Economics*, vol. CXVI, no. 3 (2001), pp. 1163-1114.

[59] On average, 25% lived in extended family settings in the 1987 to 1996 period. Just following welfare reform, the share living in extended families increased to 30% in 1998 and 33% in 1999, and then to an average of 28% from 2000 to 2009. Based on CRS estimates from U.S. Census Bureau 1988 to 2010 CPS/ASEC data. (See Table C-14 for supporting data.)

[60] In 2009, for example, 20% of nonworking single mothers were living with other unrelated family members, of which over four fifths were designated as "cohabiting partners." In comparison, about 9% of nonworking single mothers lived with unrelated family members in 1987. Based on CRS estimates from U.S. Census Bureau 1988 to 2010 CPS/ASEC data.

[61] The self reporting of "illness or disability" on the CPS/ASEC as the reason for not working may also be suspect if, as a greater share of mothers have gone to work, the attribution of "taking care of home or family" as the reason for not working has become less socially acceptable for not working, especially among mothers who receive welfare benefits.

[62] CRS Report R41625, *Federal Benefits and Services for People with Low Income: Programs, Policy, and Spending, FY2008-FY2009*, by Karen Spar.

[63] For a discussion of issues relating to the TANF, see CRS Report R41781, *The Temporary Assistance for Needy Families Block Grant: Issues for the 112th Congress*, by Gene Falk.

[64] For summary of the legislative history of the Aid to Families with Dependent Children, see http://www.acf.hhs.gov/ programs/ofa/policy/legisum.htm. Also, CRS Report 84-546 EPW, *Brief legislative History of Title IV-A of the Social Security Act: Grants to States for Aid to Families with Dependent Children (AFDC)*, by Vee Burke, February 24, 1984 (archived report, available to congressional clients upon request).

[65] Mark H. Leff, "Consensus for Reform: The Mothers'-Pension Movement in the Progressive Era," *The Social Service Review*, vol. 47, no. 3 (September 1973), pp. 397-417.

[66] See Jane M. Hoey, "Aid to Families with Dependent Children," *Annals of the American Academy of Political and Social Science, Appraising the Social Security Program*, vol. 202 (March 1939), pp. 76-78

[67] Mark H. Leff, op. cit., p. 402.

[68] Missouri and Illinois were the first states to establish mothers' pensions, in 1911. By 1913, 20 states had mothers' pensions, and by 1919, 39 states and the territories of Alaska and Hawaii had mothers' pensions. In 1931, every state except for Georgia and South Carolina had mothers' pensions. See Michael B. Katz, *In the Shadow of the Poorhouse: A Social History of Welfare in America* (New York, NY: Basic Books, 1996), p. 133.

[69] See Legislative History, Social Security Act of 1935, on the Internet at *http://www.ssa.gov /history/35activ.html*.

[70] The federal maximum payment amounted to $6 per month for the first child in a family, plus $4 per month for each additional child. The federal matching rate of state AFDC expenditures would grow over time.

[71] See U.S. Department of Health and Human Services, Assistant Secretary for Planning and Evaluation, *A Brief History of the AFDC Program,* available on the Internet at http://aspe.hhs.gov/hsp/AFDC/baseline/1history.pdf.

[72] Jane M. Hoey, "Aid to Families with Dependent Children," *Annals of the American Academy of Political and Social Science, Appraising the Social Security Program*, vol. 202 (March 1939), pp. 76, 78.

[73] Linda Gordon, *Pitied But Not Entitled: Single Mothers and the History of Welfare, 1890-1935* (New York: The Free Press, 1994), p. 21.

[74] Mimi Abramovitz, *Regulating the Lives of Women: Social Welfare Policy form Colonial Times to Present* (Boston: South End Press, 1988), p. 321.

[75] Ibid., p. 76.

[76] For an in depth discussion, see for example: Martha Derthick, *The Influence of Federal Grants, Public Assistance in Massachusetts* (Cambridge, MA: Harvard University Press).

[77] See http://www.ssa.gov/history/1940.html.

[78] Under 1958 amendments to the Social Security Act, federal ADC payments to states were no longer based on individual assistance payments, but on total state expenditures, which were matched within an average payment per recipient. The federal matching percent could be no less than 50% and no greater than 65%. Under 1965 Amendments to the act, the federal matching rate grew to a minimum of 50% and a maximum of 83% of expenditures, which varied by state, depending on an inverse relationship of state per capita income relative to U.S. per capita income. See http://www.acf.hhs.gov/programs/ofa/policy/legisum.htm.

[79] James T. Patterson, *America's Struggle Against Poverty, 1900-1985* (Cambridge, MA: Harvard University Press, 1986), p. 181.

[80] Francis Fox Piven and Richard A. Cloward, *Poor People's Movements, Why They Succeed, How They Fail* (New York: Vintage Books, 1979), pp. 264-361.

[81] Abramovitz, op. cit., p. 335.

[82] See for example, Daniel P. Moynihan, *The Politics of a Guaranteed Income: The Nixon Administration and the Family Assistance Plan* (New York: Random House, 1973), p. 25.

[83] Ibid., p. 334.

[84] Patterson, op. cit., p. 179.

[85] John T. Woolley and Gerhard Peters, Statement by the President Upon Approving the Public Welfare Amendments Bill, July 26, 1962, The American Presidency Project [online]. Santa Barbara, CA. Available on the Internet at http://www.presidency.ucsb.edu/ws/?pid=8788.

[86] A case worker was to carry no more than 60 cases and no supervisor to have more than five workers. President's Commission on Income Maintenance Programs, *Background Papers*, 1970, pp. 299-309.

[87] See Martha Derthick, *Uncontrollable Spending for Social Services Grants* (Washington, DC: The Brookings Institution, 1975).

[88] For a brief discussion of the separation of social services from income maintenance, see Mark E. Courtney et al., "Comparing Welfare and Child Welfare Populations: An Argument for Rethinking the Safety Net," in *Child Welfare Research: Advances for Practice and Policy*, ed. Duncan Lindsey and Aron Shlonsky (New York: Oxford University Press, 2008), pp. 273-275.

[89] Vee Burke, op. cit., p. 7.

[90] Ibid., p. 7. For a more detailed discussion see Library of Congress Legislative Reference Service Report (HV 84 D, ED-372), *The Limitation on Federal Matching in the Aid to Families with Dependent Children Program – The So-Called AFDC Freeze*, by William Fullerton, April 1, 1969 (archived report, available by request).

[91] The 1967 amendments also restructured title IV (Grants to States for Aid to Families with Dependent Children) of the act into parts: with Part A—AFDC; Part B—Child Welfare Services (a new part, transferred from title V, and revised; and a new Part C—Work Incentive Program (WIN), discussed later. Vee Burke, op. cit., p. 6.

[92] Ibid., pp. 7-8.

[93] Ibid., p. 4.

[94] Ibid., p. 4.

[95] U.S. Department of Health and Human Services, Assistant Secretary for Planning and Evaluation, *A Brief History of the AFDC Program,* available on the Internet at http://aspe.hhs.gov/hsp/AFDC/baseline/1history.pdf.

[96] Mildred Rein, "Social Services as a Work Strategy," *The Social Service Review*, vol. 49, no. 4 (December 1975), pp. 515-538.

[97] Section 1115 of the Social Security Act, established in 1962, grants the Secretary authority to waive compliance of states with certain sections of the Social Security Act for state experiments or demonstrations that the Secretary judges to promote specific objectives of the act. For a discussion of waiver authority under this section, see U.S. Department of Health and Human Services, Assistant Secretary for Planning and Evaluation, *State Welfare Waivers: An Overview*, available on the Internet at http://aspe.hhs.gov/hsp/isp/waiver2 /waivers.htm.

[98] The CPS estimates are for all adults reporting receipt of AFDC or TANF during the year, converted to an estimate of an annual monthly average, based on the number of months over the year recipients reported receiving assistance. For a detailed discussion of cash welfare under-reporting on the CPS and other surveys see Richard Bavier, *Accounting for increases in failure to report AFDC/TANF receipt*, Office of Management and Budget, Unpublished manuscript, Washington, DC, 2000.

In: Trends in the Economic Well-Being … ISBN: 978-1-62100-931-3
Eds.: G. Young and D. T. Green © 2012 Nova Science Publishers, Inc.

Chapter 2

TEMPORARY ASSISTANCE FOR NEEDY FAMILIES: IMPLICATIONS OF CASELOAD AND PROGRAM CHANGES FOR FAMILIES AND PROGRAM MONITORING

Kay E. Brown

WHY GAO DID THIS STUDY

The Temporary Assistance for Needy Families (TANF) program, created in 1996, is one of the key federal funding streams provided to states to assist women and children in poverty. A critical aspect of TANF has been its focus on employment and self-sufficiency, and the primary means to measure state efforts in this area has been TANF's work participation rate requirements. Legislative changes in 2005 were generally expected to strengthen these work requirements. Given changes in the number of families participating in TANF over time and questions about whether the program is achieving its goals, this testimony draws on previous GAO work to focus on 1) key changes to state welfare programs made in response to TANF and other legislation and their effect on caseload trends; 2) how low-income single-parent families are faring; and 3) how recent developments in state programs and the economy may affect federal monitoring of TANF. To address these issues, in previous work conducted from November 2008 to May 2010, GAO analyzed state data reported to the Department of Health and Human Services; used microsimulation analyses; surveyed state TANF administrators in 50 states and the District of Columbia; interviewed officials in 21 states selected to represent a range of economic conditions and TANF policy decisions; conducted site visits to Florida, Ohio, and Oregon; and reviewed relevant federal laws, regulations, and research.

What GAO Found

Changes states made to their welfare programs as they implemented TANF contributed to a significant decline in program participation, but caseloads are starting to increase in many states. The strong economy of the 1990s, TANF's focus on work, and other factors contributed to increased family incomes and a decline in the number of families poor enough to be eligible for cash assistance. However, research shows that state policies—including TANF work requirements, time limits, and sanction and diversion policies—also contributed to the caseload decline, as fewer eligible families participated in the program. In recent years, states have varied in their response to changes in economic conditions, with caseloads rising in 37 states and falling in 13 states between December 2007 and September 2009, the latest data available when we did our work.

Like TANF recipients, families who left TANF, as well as those who qualified for the program but who did not participate, had low incomes and continued to rely on other government supports. In the years following welfare reform, many of the parents who left cash assistance found employment, and some were better off than they were on welfare, but earnings were typically low and many worked in unstable, low-wage jobs with few benefits. Among eligible families who did not participate, a small subset did not work and had very low incomes.

Efforts to measure states' engagement of TANF recipients in work activities and to monitor states' use of all TANF funds have been of limited use in ensuring accountability for meeting federal TANF goals, according to our analysis. Work participation rates—a key performance measure for TANF, as currently measured and reported, do not appear to be achieving the intended purpose of encouraging states to engage specified proportions of TANF recipients in work activities. In addition, states' decisions to shift their spending from cash assistance to other programs and work supports such as childcare have highlighted gaps in the information available at the federal level on how many families received TANF services and how states used funds to meet TANF goals.

A central feature of the TANF block grant is the flexibility it provides to states to design and implement welfare programs tailored to address their own circumstances, but this flexibility must be balanced with mechanisms to ensure state programs are held accountable for meeting program goals. The limited usefulness of current measures of work participation and the lack of information on how states use funds to aid families and to meet TANF goals hinders decision makers in considering the success of TANF and what trade offs might be involved in any changes to TANF when it is reauthorized.

Mr. Chairman and Members of the Committee:

I am pleased to have the opportunity to participate in today's discussion of women in poverty. I will focus on the role of the Temporary Assistance for Needy Families (TANF) program in providing assistance to this population. As you know, many families receiving TANF cash assistance are headed by single parents, and because the vast majority of those parents are women, the $16.5 billion TANF block grant is one of the key federal funding streams provided to states to assist women and children in poverty. The Bureau of the Census just released last week poverty statistics for 2009 and the poverty rate for children is now at 20.7 percent, the highest it has been this decade. My remarks today are mainly based on two of our recent reports entitled *TANF: Fewer Eligible Families Have Received Cash Assistance Since the 1990s, and the Recession's Impact on Caseloads Varies by State*; and *TANF: Implications of Recent Legislative and Economic Changes for State Programs and Work Participation Rates.*[1]

As you know, the Personal Responsibility and Work Opportunity Reconciliation Act of 1996 (PRWORA) introduced sweeping changes to federal welfare policy. PRWORA ended Aid to Families with Dependent Children (AFDC), which entitled eligible families to monthly cash payments, and created TANF, a capped block grant that emphasizes employment and work supports for most families who receive cash assistance. Under the TANF block grant program, states receive a capped amount of federal funds to design and operate their own welfare programs within federal guidelines. The Department of Health and Human Services (HHS) administers the TANF program, which provides states with up to about $16.5 billion each year in TANF block grant funds, and each state must contribute a specified level of its own funds to qualify for the grant. Within certain limitations, states set their own eligibility limits and benefit levels for cash recipients, but they must restrict most families to a lifetime limit of 60 months of federally funded TANF cash assistance. Central to TANF's focus on employment and self-sufficiency are TANF's work participation rate requirements, which require states to involve a minimum percentage of their families receiving TANF cash assistance in work activities for a required number of hours each week.

Recently, several legislative and economic changes have affected TANF. First, with the reauthorization of the TANF block grant through the Deficit Reduction Act of 2005 (DRA), the Congress took steps generally expected to strengthen TANF work requirements by modifying the credit provided to states for reducing the number of families receiving TANF. Following DRA, the U.S. economy experienced a severe recession and, in response, the Congress passed the American Recovery and Reinvestment Act of 2009 (Recovery Act) which included provisions affecting TANF such as the creation of a $5 billion Emergency Contingency Fund for state TANF programs. States qualify for this fund based on increases in expenditures for short –term non-recurrent benefits or subsidized employment or increases in the number of families receiving cash assistance. This fund supplemented the TANF contingency fund, which under PRWORA had made up to $2 billion available to states.

With the creation of TANF, the number of families who received cash assistance fell significantly, from 4.8 million families on average each month in 1995—just prior to the creation of TANF—to 1.7 million in 2008. More recently, however, caseloads have begun to rise in some states. Recent changes in state TANF programs made in response to DRA as well as changes in the economy have raised questions about how the program has affected low-income families over time and how best to monitor TANF's progress in meeting two of its key goals—to provide assistance to needy families so that children may be cared for in their own homes or in the homes of relatives and to end the dependence of needy families on government benefits by promoting job preparation, work, and marriage.

My remarks today—based primarily on our February and May 2010 reports—will focus on the following three issues: (1) key changes made to state welfare programs in response to TANF and other legislation and the effect of these changes on caseload trends; (2) how single parent families with children are faring, including those who receive TANF cash assistance as well as those who are eligible but do not receive assistance; and (3) the implications of recent developments on monitoring state TANF programs.

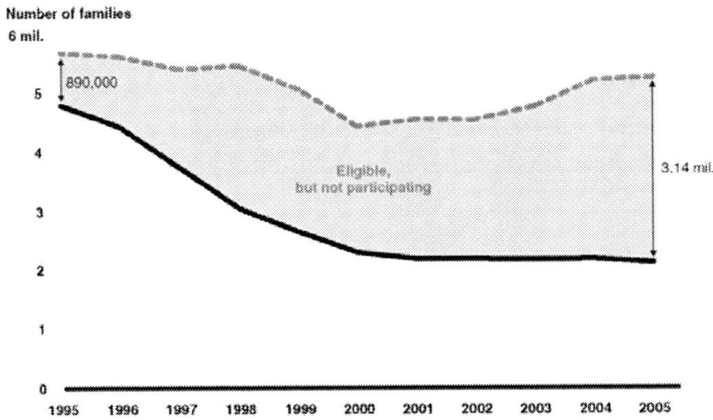

- - - - Eligible for AFDC or TANF Cash Assistance Programs

—— Participating in AFDC or TANF Cash Assistance Programs

Source: GAO analysis of data from HHS's *Indicators of Welfare Dependence* , based on the TRIM3 model.

Note: For estimates of families' eligibility and participation using TRIM3, 2005 was the latest data that was publicly available when we conducted our work. TRIM3 is a microsimulation model funded by HHS that simulates major governmental tax, transfer, and health programs.

Figure 1. Families Estimated as Eligible for and Participating in Cash Assistance through the AFDC or TANF Cash Assistance Programs, Monthly Average, by Calendar Year, 1995 through 2005.

We used multiple methodologies to develop our findings for these reports. We reviewed and analyzed state TANF data reported to HHS; reported on microsimulation analyses conducted for us by the Urban Institute using a model known as TRIM3[2]; reviewed relevant federal laws, regulations, and guidance and relevant research on the factors affecting the decline of cash recipient families; interviewed HHS officials; surveyed state TANF administrators from the 50 states and Washington, D.C.; interviewed TANF officials in 21 states, and conducted site visits to meet with state and local TANF officials in Florida, Ohio, and Oregon. The states we selected for interviews and site visits had a range of economic conditions, caseloads, TANF policies, and geographic diversity. We assessed the data we received for data reliability and concluded that the data were sufficiently reliable for the purposes of our report.

We conducted our work from November 2008 to May 2010 in accordance with all sections of GAO's Quality Assurance Framework that are relevant to our objectives. The framework requires that we plan and perform the engagement to obtain sufficient and appropriate evidence to meet our stated objectives and to discuss any limitations in our work. We believe that the information and data obtained, and the analysis conducted, provide a reasonable basis for any findings and conclusions in this product.

Changes to State TANF Programs Contributed to a Long-Term Decline in Participation but Caseloads Are Starting to Increase in Many States

In response to the creation of TANF, states implemented more work-focused welfare programs, and research shows that these changes—in concert with other policy changes and economic conditions—contributed to raising the incomes of single parent families so that fewer were eligible for cash assistance. In designing and implementing their new TANF programs, states focused more than ever before on helping welfare recipients and other low-income parents find jobs. Many states implemented work-focused programs that stressed moving parents quickly into jobs and structured the benefits to allow more parents to combine welfare and work.[3] States also imposed financial consequences, or sanctions, on families that did not comply with TANF work or other requirements, strengthening the incentives for TANF participants to comply with work requirements. Other concurrent policy changes contributed to an increase in the share of single parents in the labor force. These included an increase in the Earned Income Tax Credit (EITC) in the 1990s and increases in the minimum wage in 1996 and 1997, both of which contributed to an increase in the returns to work. Additional funds for federal and state work supports such as child care also made it easier for single parents to enter the labor force. Finally, the strong economy of the 1990s facilitated the move from welfare to work for many TANF recipients. A decline in the unemployment rate and strong economic growth contributed to the widespread availability of job openings for workers of all skill levels in many parts of the country. During this period, labor force participation increased among single mothers, the population most affected by TANF—from 58 percent in 1995—the year prior to the creation of TANF—to 71 percent in 2007, with most of this increase occurring immediately following the passage of welfare reform. Because the incomes of many single-parent families increased as a result of these policies, in total, 420,000 fewer families had incomes low enough to be eligible for cash assistance in 2005 compared to 1995, according to HHS data.

At the same time that some families worked more and had higher incomes, others had income that left them still eligible for TANF cash assistance; however, many of these eligible families were not participating in the program. According to our estimates, the vast majority—87 percent—of the caseload decline can be explained by the decline in eligible families participating in the program, in part because of changes to state welfare programs. (See Figure 1). These changes include mandatory work requirements, changes to application procedures, lower benefits, and policies such as lifetime limits on assistance, diversion policies, and sanctions for non-compliance, according to a review of the research.

While mandatory work activities assisted some participants in getting jobs, according to a research synthesis conducted for HHS, these mandates may have led other families to choose not to apply rather than be expected to fulfill the requirement to work. Other families may have found it more difficult to apply for or continue to participate in the program, especially those with poor mental or physical health or other characteristics that make employment difficult. A decline in average cash benefits may also have contributed to the decline in participation. Average cash benefits under 2005 TANF rules were 17 percent lower than they were under 1995 AFDC rules, according to our TRIM3 estimates, as cash benefit levels in many states have not been updated or kept pace with inflation. Research also suggests that in response to lifetime limits on the amount of time a family can receive cash assistance eligible families may hold off on applying for cash assistance and "bank" their time, a practice that could contribute to the decline in families' use of cash assistance. In addition, fewer families may have applied or completed applications for TANF cash assistance because of state policies and practices for diverting applicants from cash assistance; nearly all states have at least one type of diversion strategy, such as the use of one-time nonrecurring benefits instead of monthly cash assistance. Finally, some studies and researchers noted that full sanctions for families noncompliance—those that cut off all benefits for a period of time—are associated with declines in the number of families receiving cash assistance, although more research is needed to validate this association.

During the recent economic recession, caseloads increased in some states but decreased in others, as circumstances in individual states as well as states' responses to the economic conditions varied. Between December 2007 and

September 2009, 37 states had increases in the number of families receiving TANF cash assistance while 13 states had decreases. However, the degree of change in families receiving TANF cash assistance varied significantly by state, as some states experienced caseload increases or decreases of over 25 percent while others experienced minimal changes of 0 to 5 percent. Nationwide, the total number of families receiving TANF cash assistance increased by 6 percent during this time period although the subset of two-parent families receiving such assistance increased by 57 percent. Initially few states reported reducing TANF-related spending on family and/or work supports in response to the recession, instead using funding sources such as the Emergency Contingency Fund created by the Recovery Act to respond to rising caseloads and/or to establish or expand subsidized employment programs. However, through their comments on our national survey and during our site visits, state officials discussed how the economic recession has caused changes to local TANF service delivery in some states. A majority of state TANF officials nationwide, as well as TANF officials from all eight localities we visited, reported that they made changes in local offices' TANF service delivery because of the economic recession.[4] Specifically, of the 31 states reporting such changes through our survey, 22 had reduced the number of TANF staff, 11 had reduced work hours at offices, and 7 had reduced the number of offices.[5] Officials in all three states we visited also reported that local TANF caseworkers are now managing an increased number of TANF cash assistance families per person. As a result of these increased caseloads, along with tightened resources, local officials in all three of the states we visited expressed their concerns that staff are less able to provide services to meet TANF cash assistance families' needs and move them toward self-sufficiency.

MOST TANF PARTICIPANTS AND ELIGIBLE NON-RECIPIENTS HAVE LOW INCOMES, AND A SMALL SUBGROUP HAVE VERY LOW INCOMES

Research on how families are faring after welfare reform has shown that, like those who receive TANF cash assistance, families that have left welfare, either for work or for other reasons, tend to remain low income and most depend in part on other public benefits. As we noted in a 2005 report, most of the parents who left cash welfare found employment and some were better off than they were on welfare, but earnings were typically low and many worked in unstable, low-wage jobs with few benefits and advancement opportunities.[6] There is evidence that some former TANF recipients have had better outcomes; for example, a 2009 study found that, in general, former TANF recipients in three cities, especially those who had left TANF prior to 2001, had higher employment rates and average income levels than they had while they were on TANF. [7] However, even among working families, many rely on government supports such as the EITC, Medicaid, the Supplemental Nutrition Assistance Program (SNAP), formerly known as the Food Stamp Program, and other programs to help support their families and lift them out of poverty, as most parents who recently left welfare are not earning enough to be self-supporting. In addition, a considerable body of work has documented families who are often described as "disconnected" from the workforce. It is not yet known whether or to what extent the recession has led to an increase in the number of these families.

A recent GAO analysis of the characteristics of low-income families several years post-welfare reform found that while families who were receiving TANF cash assistance in 2005 had low incomes, a third worked full-time and most received other public supports, according to the most recent data available. The median household income of families receiving TANF cash assistance was $9,606 per year, not including means-tested benefits. One third of families who received TANF cash assistance at some point during the year (33 percent) were engaged in full-time employment, while 44 percent were headed by an adult without earnings. About a fifth (18 percent) of these families were headed by an adult who had a work-limiting disability. The vast majority of families receiving TANF cash assistance—91 percent—also received at least one other public benefit, with most (88 percent) receiving benefits from the Supplemental Nutritional Assistance Program (SNAP), formerly known as the Food Stamp Program, and a smaller proportion receiving subsidized housing (22 percent), child care subsidized by the Child Care and Development Fund (CCDF) (11 percent), or Supplemental Security Income (SSI), a cash assistance program for low-income people with disabilities (22 percent). Only 16 percent of families receiving cash assistance included married couples, and even fewer—less than 10 percent—had income from an unmarried partner.

Many TANF eligible families do not participate in the program, possibly because they left the program or because they did not apply. Our analysis found that on average, these families had higher incomes than TANF recipients, but median incomes remained low, a significant proportion did not work full time, and many received public supports other than TANF. Compared to TANF cash assistance recipients, eligible non-recipients had higher median incomes ($15,000 per year) and higher rates of full-time employment (44 percent). However, a significant proportion of TANF-eligible non-recipient families—41 percent—were headed by an adult without any earnings, and 11 percent had a work limiting disability. A somewhat lower percentage of those eligible but not receiving TANF cash assistance received other public benefits (66 percent received any benefit), but a majority lived in households that received SNAP (59 percent). Receipt of other benefits was also somewhat lower than among TANF recipients, with 13 percent receiving subsidized housing, 8 percent receiving CCDF-subsidized child care, and 18 percent receiving SSI. More eligible non-participating families were headed by married couples than participating families, but no more had income from an unmarried partner.

A small subgroup of families eligible for but not receiving TANF cash assistance (732,000 families in 2005), did not work and did not receive SSI benefits and this group has lower incomes than TANF recipients and other eligible non-recipients. In addition, these families also had lower receipt of other public benefits compared to TANF recipients. Among families with no earned income that received neither TANF nor SSI, the median income from all sources was $7,020, an amount equal to about 45 percent of the federal poverty threshold for a family consisting of one adult and two children. Twelve percent of this group of families was headed by a parent who reported having a work-limiting disability. The extent to which these families received other public benefits was similar to that of other families eligible but not participating in TANF, with 66 percent receiving any benefit. Most (63 percent) received SNAP benefits while 18 percent received subsidized housing, and 4 percent received CCDF-subsidized child care. These more disadvantaged non-participants accounted for 11 percent of all families who were eligible for TANF cash assistance in 2005.

Efforts to Measure States' Engagement of TANF Recipients in Work Activities and to Monitor States' Use of All TANF Funds Fall Short

Data on caseload trends, state policies, and how families are faring can provide important insight into how TANF programs are working. However, work participation rates—a key accountability feature of TANF, as currently measured and reported—do not appear to be achieving the intended purpose of encouraging states to engage specified proportions of TANF adults in work activities. In addition, as cash assistance caseloads fell, many states shifted their spending away from cash assistance toward work supports such as child care, highlighting information gaps at the federal level in how many families received TANF services and how states used federal and state MOE funds to meet TANF goals.

States Used Flexibilities Allowed in Law to Engage a Smaller Share of Participants in Work Activities than Stated Goal

To promote TANF's focus on work, HHS measures state performance by the proportion of TANF participants engaged in allowable work activities. States are expected to ensure that at least 50 percent of all families receiving TANF cash assistance participate in one or more of 12 categories of work activities[8] for an average of 30 hours per week.[9] PRWORA established penalties for states that did not meet their required work participation rates and gave HHS the authority to make determinations regarding these penalties.

However, states can take advantage of program options to make it easier to meet their required rates. For example, states can annually apply to HHS for a caseload reduction credit that generally decreased the state's required work participation rates by the same percentage that the state's caseload decreased since a specified year, established as 1995 in PRWORA.[10] Because of the significant drop in caseload size, many states were able to reduce their required work participation rate. In fact, 18 states reported caseload reductions of at least 50 percent in fiscal year 2006, effectively reducing their required work participation rate to zero. In addition, states can modify the calculation of their work participation rates by funding certain families with state maintenance-of-effort (MOE) dollars[11] rather than federal TANF block grant dollars. By using state MOE dollars rather than federal dollars, states are able to remove these families from the work participation rate calculation. Between 2001 and 2006, all but two states met the participation rate requirement, according to HHS data.[12] However, nationally, between 31 and 34 percent of families receiving cash assistance met their work requirements during this time.

In 2006, DRA reauthorized the TANF block grant through fiscal year 2010 and made several modifications that were generally expected to strengthen TANF work requirements intended to help more families attain self-sufficiency, and to improve data reliability.[13] For example, DRA modified the caseload reduction credit by changing the base year from 1995 to 2005, and it mandated that families receiving cash assistance funded with state maintenance of effort dollars be included in the calculation of the work participation rates. It also directed HHS to issue regulations defining the 12 work activities and included new requirements to better ensure the reliability of work participation rate data.

We found that the proportion of families receiving TANF cash assistance that met work participation requirements has changed little since DRA was enacted and is still below the 50 percent generally specified as the required rate. In fiscal years 2007 and 2008—the two years following DRA for which national data are available—between 29 and 30 percent of families receiving TANF cash assistance met their work requirements.[14] In numbers of families, 243,000 of 816,000 families met their work requirements in fiscal year 2008. The small decrease in the proportion of families that met their requirements after DRA may be related, in part, to the federal work activity definitions and tightened work hour reporting and verification procedures states had to comply with after the act, as well as states' ability to make the required changes.[15]

The types of work activities in which families receiving TANF cash assistance most frequently participated were similar before and after DRA. For example, among families that met their work requirements, the majority participated in unsubsidized employment in the years both before and after DRA. In all of the years analyzed, the next most frequent work activities were job search and job readiness assistance, vocational educational training, and work experience. [16]

Although the national rate did not change significantly, fewer states met the required work participation rates after DRA, according to HHS data.[17] As before DRA, states used a variety of options and strategies to meet their required work participation rate. For example:

- States continued to request caseload reduction credits to help lower their required work participation rates; however, the credits were significantly smaller after DRA, since caseloads went down less after 2005.
- Some states lowered their required rates by spending state MOE dollars in excess of what is required under federal law on TANF-related programs[18] – a practice we found enabled 22 states to meet their rates in 2007 and 14 states in 2008.[19] Total state MOE

expenditures increased by almost $2 billion between fiscal years 2006 and 2008, which appears to be related to state spending on programs and services such as preventing and reducing out-of-wedlock pregnancies.

- Some states used policies to ensure that families complying with their individual work requirements were included in the work participation rate calculation by, for example providing monthly cash assistance to working families previously on TANF or about to lose TANF eligibility because their working incomes placed them just above eligibility thresholds. 18 states have implemented such programs since DRA.
- In contrast, after DRA required that state maintenance of effort dollars be included in the calculation of the work participation rates, some states removed certain nonworking families from the calculation of their rates by funding cash assistance for these families with state dollars unconnected to the TANF program – a practice we found in 29 states. We learned that states often use these state-funded programs to provide cash assistance to families that typically have the most difficulty meeting the TANF work requirements, such as families with a disabled member or recent immigrants and refugees.

In short, because of the various factors that affect the calculation of states' work participation rates, the rate's usefulness as an indicator of a state's effort to help participants achieve self-sufficiency is limited. Moreover, the rate does not allow for clear comparisons across state TANF programs or comparisons of individual state programs over time. This is the same conclusion we reached in our 2005 report that triggered some of the DRA changes to improve this measure of states' performance. Further, our 2005 review before DRA changes as well as the one we just completed in May of this year indicate that the TANF work rate requirements as enacted, in combination with the flexibility provided, may not serve as an incentive for states to engage more families or to work with families with complex needs. Many states have cited challenges in meeting work performance standards under DRA, such as new requirements to verify participants' actual activity hours and certain limitations on the types and timing of activities that count toward meeting the requirements. The TANF work rate requirements—as established in the original legislation and revised in the Deficit Reduction Act—may not yet have achieved the appropriate balance between flexibility for states and accountability for federal TANF goals.

Reduced Cash Assistance Caseloads Freed up TANF Funds for Purposes Beyond Welfare-to-Work Programs but Limited Information Exists on Use of These Funds

The substantial decline in traditional cash assistance caseloads combined with state spending flexibilities under the TANF block grant allowed states to broaden their use of TANF funds. As a result, TANF and MOE dollars played an increasing role in state budgets outside of traditional cash assistance payments. In our 2006 report that reviewed state budgets in nine states,[20] we found that in the decade since Congress created TANF, the states used their federal and state TANF-related funds throughout their budgets for low-income individuals, supporting a wide range of state priorities, such as refundable state earned income credits for the working poor, prekindergarten, child welfare services, mental health, and substance abuse services, among others. While some of this spending, such as that for child care assistance, relates directly to helping cash assistance recipients leave and stay off the welfare rolls, other spending is directed to a broader population that did not necessarily ever receive welfare payments.. This is in keeping with the broad purposes of TANF specified in the law:

1. providing assistance so that children could be cared for in their own homes or in the homes of relatives;
2. ending families' dependence on government benefits by promoting job preparation, work, and marriage;
3. preventing and reducing the incidence of out-of-wedlock pregnancies; and:
4. encouraging the formation and maintenance of two-parent families.

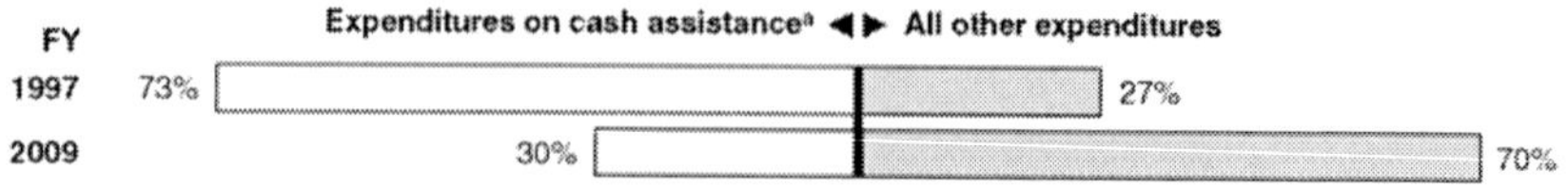

Source: GAO analysis of HHS TANF expenditure data.

Note: Expenditures for both cash assistance and other purposes totaled $19.0 billion in fiscal year 1997 and $30.6 billion in fiscal year 2009. The fiscal year 2009 data include Recovery Act spending of $550 million. Excluding Recovery Act spending does not change the percentages.

Figure 2. Expenditures for Cash Assistance and Other Purposes, Fiscal Years 1997 and 2009.

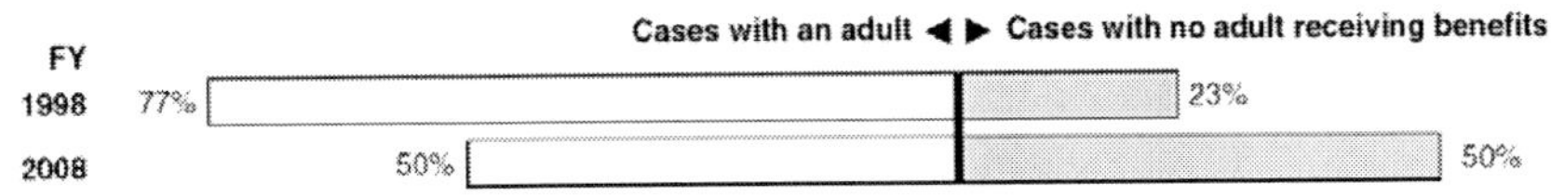

Source: GAO analysis of HHS data.

Figure 3. Proportion of Child-Only Families Receiving Cash Assistance, Fiscal Year 1998 and Fiscal Year 2008.

More recent data indicated that this trend has continued, even under recessionary conditions. In fiscal year 2009, federal TANF and state MOE expenditures for purposes other than cash assistance[21] totaled 70 percent of all expenditures compared with 27 percent in fiscal year 1997, when states first implemented TANF, as shown in figure 2. In addition, of the 21 states we surveyed for our February 2010 report, few reported that they had reduced federal TANF and MOE spending for other purposes, such as child care and subsidized employment programs, to offset increased expenditures for growth in their cash assistance caseloads. States that increased spending on cash assistance while maintaining or increasing spending for other purposes did so by spending reserve funds, accessing the TANF Contingency Fund, accessing the TANF Emergency Contingency Fund created by the Recovery Act, or a combination of the three.[22]

This shift in spending left gaps in the information gathered at the federal level to ensure state accountability. Because existing oversight mechanisms focus on cash assistance, which no longer accounts for the majority of TANF and MOE spending, we may be missing important information on the total numbers served and how states use TANF funds to help families to achieve program goals in ways beyond their welfare-to-work programs. For example, states have used significant portions of their TANF funds to augment their child care subsidy programs, which often serve non-TANF families, yet we do not know how many children are served or what role these subsidies play in helping low-income families avoid welfare dependency, a key TANF goal. Further, many states use TANF funds to fund a significant portion of their child welfare programs. In effect, there is little information on the numbers of people served by TANF-funded programs other than cash assistance, and there is no real measure of workload or of how services supported by TANF and MOE funds meet the goals of welfare reform.

Another implication of changing caseloads relates to their changing composition, with about half of the families receiving cash assistance composed of cases with no adult receiving assistance in fiscal year 2008 compared with less than one-quarter in fiscal year 1998 (see Figure3). There are four main categories of "child-only" cases: (1) the parent is disabled and receiving SSI; (2) the parent is a noncitizen and therefore ineligible; (3) the child is living with a nonparent relative; and (4) the parent has been sanctioned and removed from cash assistance for failing to comply with program requirements, and the family's benefit has been correspondingly reduced. These families, with parents or guardians not receiving TANF cash assistance and generally not subject to work requirements, have not been the focus of efforts to help families achieve self-sufficiency.

Concluding Observations

Nearly 15 years after the creation of TANF, the expected upcoming reauthorization of the program has brought renewed interest to efforts to assess how well the program is meeting the needs of low income families with children—most headed by women—and putting them on a path to self-sufficiency. While the dramatic decline in the TANF caseload following welfare reform and the increase in employment among single mothers has been cited as evidence for the program's success, questions have been raised about its effect on families. Many who left the rolls transitioned to low wage, unstable jobs, and research has shown that a small subset of families who neither receive TANF nor earn income may have been left behind. Following the recent economic recession, poverty among children has climbed to its highest level in years.

A central feature of the TANF block grant is the flexibility it provides to states to design and implement welfare programs tailored to address their own circumstances, but this flexibility must be balanced with mechanisms to ensure state programs are held accountable for meeting program goals. Over time we have learned that states' success in engaging TANF cash assistance recipients in the type, hours, and levels of work activities specified in the law has, in many cases, been limited, though they have met the required targets using the flexibility allowed. Although the DRA changes to TANF work requirements were expected to strengthen the work participation rate as a performance measure and move more families toward self-sufficiency, the proportion of TANF recipients engaged in work activities remains unchanged. States' use of the modifications allowed in federal law and regulations, as well as states' policy choices, have diminished the rates' usefulness as the national performance measure for TANF, and shown it to be limited as an incentive for states to engage more families or work with families with complex needs. Furthermore, while states have devoted significant amounts of the block grant funds as well as state funds to other activities, little is known about use of these funds. Lack of information on how states use these funds to aid families and to meet TANF goals hinders decision makers in considering the success of TANF and what trade offs might be involved in any changes to TANF when it is reauthorized.

We provided a draft of the reports we drew on for this testimony to HHS for its review, and copies of the agency's written responses can be found in the appendices of the relevant reports. In its comments, HHS generally said that the reports were informative and did not disagree with our findings.

Mr. Chairman, this concludes my statement. I would be pleased to respond to any questions you or other Members of the Committee may have.

End Notes

[1] See GAO-10-164 (Washington, D.C.: February 23, 2010) and GAO-10-525 (Washington, D.C.: May 28, 2010).

[2] TRIM3 is maintained and developed at the Urban Institute under primary funding from HHS, Office of the Assistant Secretary for Planning and Evaluation. Using TRIM3 for these analyses required our input on assumptions and/or interpretations about economic behavior and the rules governing federal programs. Therefore, the conclusions presented in this testimony are attributable only to GAO.

[3] Not all TANF families are subject to work requirements. TANF law allows states to exclude single custodial parents caring for a child under the age of 1, for example. Families without adult recipients—child-only cases—are sometimes exempt from work requirements and time limits. States also have the option to consider some parents not "work eligible," such as those on SSI or Social Security Disability Insurance.

[4] For more information on the eight localities we visited, see appendix I of GAO-10-525.

[5] In contrast, 5 states reported that they had increased the number of TANF staff, 4 had increased work hours at offices, and 1 had increased the number of offices.

[6] GAO, *Welfare Reform: More Information Needed to Assess Promising Strategies to Increase Parents' Incomes,* GAO-06-108 (Washington, D.C.: Dec. 2005).

[7] Bianca Frogner, Robert Moffitt, David Ribar, *Income, Employment, and Welfare Receipt After Welfare Reform: 1999-2005 Evidence from the Three-City Study*, Johns Hopkins University Working Paper 09-02 (May 2009).

[8] For two-parent families, the participation rate is 90 percent. For illustrative purposes, we refer primarily to the expected rate for all families. For more information on two-parent TANF families, see GAO-10-525.

[9] To be counted as engaging in work for a month, most TANF families are required to participate in work activities for an average of 30 hours per week in that month. However, PRWORA defined different weekly work hour requirements for teen parents attending school, single parents of children under age 6, and two-parent families.

[10] See GAO-10-525.

[11] The $16.5 billion per year TANF block grant is a fixed federal funding stream to states, which is coupled with a maintenance-of-effort (MOE) provision that requires states to maintain a

significant portion of their historic financial commitment to their welfare programs. To meet the MOE requirement, each state must generally spend 75 or 80 percent of what it was spending in fiscal year 1994 on welfare-related programs, including: Aid to Families with Dependent Children, Job Opportunities and Basic Skills Training (JOBS), Emergency Assistance (EA), and AFDC-related child care programs.

[12] This refers to the all families rates; during this time period, from 1 to 4 states each year did not meet the higher two-parent rate.

[13] In our 2005 report on TANF work participation, we found differences in how states defined the 12 TANF work activities, which had resulted in some states counting activities that others did not count, and, therefore, an inconsistent measurement of work participation across states. We also found that some of the states in our review lacked internal controls over work participation data. See GAO, *Welfare Reform: HHS Should Exercise Oversight to Help Ensure TANF Work Participation,* GAO-05-821 (Washington, D.C.: Aug. 19, 2005).

[14] An additional 8 and 10 percent of TANF families in fiscal years 2007 and 2008, respectively, participated in work activities for less than the amount required to meet their individual work requirements. Further, some states reported TANF families participating in "other" work activities that do not count toward the federal work requirements, both before and after DRA.

[15] As noted earlier, our 2005 report found differences in how states defined the 12 TANF work activities, which had resulted in some states counting activities that others did not count, and, therefore, an inconsistent measurement of work participation across states. We also found that some of the states in our review reported the hours recipients were scheduled to work, rather than those actually worked, as work participation. As a result, some states likely needed to make significant changes to their work definitions and procedures after DRA. See GAO-05-821.

[16] We analyzed states' work participation data reported to HHS for selected years. For more information, see appendix I of GAO-10-525.

[17] In 2007, 12 states did not meet the 50 percent participation rate requirement, and in 2008, 7 states did not meet it.

[18] DRA also added a provision allowing states to count a broader range of their own expenditures toward the TANF MOE requirement. Additionally, if states spend in excess of the required MOE amount, they are allowed to reduce the number of families included in the calculation of their work participation rates through the caseload reduction credit calculation. HHS officials told us that, prior to DRA, only one state had claimed excess MOE expenditures toward its caseload reduction.

[19] Although the majority of states reported excess MOE expenditures after DRA we did not determine whether these increases reflected new state spending.

[20] See GAO-06-414.

[21] We refer to this category as cash assistance, although ACF uses the term "basic assistance." This category includes benefits designed to meet on-going basic needs, including cash, payments, or vouchers.

[22] States can save portions of their TANF block grant to use in the future for cash assistance to families. PRWORA also established a contingency fund for state TANF programs to draw on and the Recovery Act provided additional funds on a time limited basis for states to meet increasing needs.

CHAPTER SOURCES

The following chapters have been previously published:

Chapter 1 - This is an edited, reformatted and augmented version of a Congressional Research Service publication, report R41917, dated July 15, 2011.

Chapter 2 – This is an edited, reformatted and augmented version of a United States Government Accountability Office publication, report GAO-10-815T, dated September 21, 2010.

INDEX

S

T